D1700171

Manipulation and Dark Psychology:

Understand Dark Psychology Secrets and Read Body Language to Identify a Narcissist. Learn Body Language, How to Read People and Analyze Others

Readers acknowledge that the author is not engaging in the rendering of legal, financial, medical or professional advice. The content within this book has been derived from various sources. Please consult a licensed professional before attempting any techniques outlined in this book.

By reading this document, the reader agrees that under no circumstances is the author responsible for any losses, direct or indirect, which are incurred as a result of the use of information contained within this document, including, but not limited to, — errors, omissions, or inaccuracies.

Table of Contents

Introduction

The following chapters will discuss how to use your brainpower to understand and utilize the concepts of Dark Psychology. Many people will go through life without these skills, and a great many problems can be boiled down to lack of understanding. The principles at work are being used against you constantly. When a person is able to read and analyze their environment, they make life easier for themselves and others. What is often missing is the ability to tap into previously existing intuition and analytic ability. We all have the skills to invest in these psychological concepts, and it just takes practice and insight.

Each of us is perceptive animals, capable of deep observation. However, we are not always taught how to use these powers. The solution is to learn about how to make connections with our own intuition, what we observe, and what we can deduce logically. How can you do this? The following chapters will present a guide on how to adjust your expectations, apply knowledge, access your intuition, and trust yourself. By doing these things, you'll find that you gain power in your life, in relationships, and in your ventures. There are plenty of books on this subject on the market, thanks again for choosing this one! Every effort was made to ensure it is full of as much useful information as possible. Please enjoy!

Chapter 1: What is Dark Psychology?

By now, you've probably heard the term Positive Psychology. It is all the rage right now to write about positive psychology and the associated concepts. Positive psychology started as a movement in the sixties and seventies in the US. It started as a way to frame psychological concepts and skills in a positive light, with accentuating a person's abilities and solutions to problems. Positive psychology became popular because it focuses on the strengths of a person and helps them to focus on the good things in life.

This is obviously very useful to a wide swathe of the population. Think about it; when you are down and experiencing challenges, you want to be able to focus on the positive and look for a positive solution to difficult problems. This follows the cultural milieu of the sixties and seventies. This was a time when everyone was thinking about the idealistic solution to problems. The civil rights movement had mostly happened, the hippie era was in full swing, and the country was experiencing the first growing pains of a post-WWII existence. Now that we had won the war and ensured a future for our country, what were we going to do with it? There was an abundance of positive feeling, for the USA, for people who were countercultural, and there was a huge feeling of optimism.

To give a little more context on the birth of this psychology, we have to understand the era that the USA was in. After WWII, the population felt that we had conquered something that was insurmountable: the threat of communism and fascism, which had threatened to spill over into all parts of the West and East. Young men had gone to war to defend their homeland, their family, and friends. The war was fought overseas, and the feeling at home was one of quiet expectation, one of trying to get by while all the soldiers were gone. Then, when they came back, they all had kids. BY this time, people started to realize that they felt stable. They felt that there was a future for their kids in this country, one without war and struggle. There was an intrinsic hopefulness, and this brought people to live in a new way: one of optimism.

Throughout the sixties and seventies, people took this attitude to heart. They felt that they wanted to make sure that their kids were able to go to good schools and get good jobs. They felt that the USA was unbeatable, that it was the land of opportunity, and it was the best country in the world.

That was a few decades ago, and a lot has changed. Now, the USA is not seen as such a great land of opportunity. Rather, people are finding that the job market is weaker than it has been in several generations, and the USA does not feel like it will be the dominant country on a global scale as if it has been for so long. The USA has become wracked with controversy, income inequality, and so many other problems have begun to change peoples' viewpoints. No longer are we planning for a long, successful era of prosperity. Many people are struggling and do not have a prosperity mindset. Along with this comes the change of many social mores and norms. Where once there was the nuclear family, now there is a looser, broader definition of family. Once there were clear, delineated roles, and now we have lost most of those expectations.

Things are different now than they have been in the past. That's where Dark Psychology comes in.

People are not so obsessed with prosperity anymore, and they are not looking to just focus on the positives and strengths of society like Positive Psychology would have them do. People now are more interested in learning about the ways that they are mistreated or manipulated. We have become more jaded and aware of various ways that we are manipulated. There is a giant media that feeds us certain information, corporations that want us just to buy, buy, buy, and politicians who want us to follow their every instruction and goal. There are a lot of negative, manipulative messages out there, and it gets difficult to sort through what is true and necessary. There are so many ways to be manipulated. Social media has become a huge tool for people who manipulate others. We get our information, recreation, and entertainment on social media, and this has made us very susceptible to lies and deception.

Dark Psychology uses tools to analyze this manipulation and learn about it so that you can utilize it for your purposes and avoid being manipulated from others. Dark Psychology, rather than focusing on the positive and strengths of each person, is more about the weaknesses and how to bolster them. It is more concerned with being able to analyze the manipulation of others and understand how propaganda and deception are being used to make you do certain things.

In order to be able to analyze when you are being manipulated and read other people, you must begin to gain awareness around the topic of Dark Psychology. This is a field that most people know a little something about already, and when you start to learn about it, you will be able to identify certain characteristics and themes from your own life that fit into the system.

We all have encountered these personalities in our lives at some point. One common Dark Triad personality is the narcissist. These people are obsessed with themselves and have trouble placing any real weight on the plight of other people. They would rather just live with themselves and keep their emotional distance from others. When narcissist goes into a relationship, it is not for equal participation and benefit. The only benefits that the narcissist is looking forward to are the ones going straight to them.

How much does success rely on understanding Dark Psychology? It is arguable that many successful people use these tactics to propel themselves to the top of whatever food chain in which they might find themselves. The delusion of importance can lend a hand when you are trying to scale up the corporate ladder, or systems of politics.

Body language is of utmost importance. Being able to analyze other people, and their intentions and emotions will help you to be more socially dominant, confident, and able. Body language is an observable phenomenon that will allow you to surmise much more than the surface suggests. Body language, unlike verbal language, is not something that most people know how to do purposefully. It is like the unconscious speaking to you through physicality.

Dark Psychology is out there, whether you like it or not. The principles contained in Dark Psychology are being utilized, sometimes for your benefit, sometimes against your will. Only by understanding the system can you defend yourself against it. Understanding the system will allow you to break free from unwanted manipulation, and will allow you to help yourself and help others. Power is really what we are after here. The ability to read others, to have emotional intelligence, to analyze relationships and other important skills allow you to bring power to your life when it was previously lacking.

There are a few important categories of people who are very good at manipulation. Let's talk about these different types and the way that they deceive others.

The first is the Narcissist. The Narcissist is a person who loves to promote themselves and gain attention. Of course, social media sites are a spot-on way to encourage someone to be a narcissist, and they are breeding grounds for obsessive behavior in this area. Narcissists are in love with themselves, and they love to have all the attention. They are not good at truly focusing on others. They always have the underlying motive of promoting themselves.

The next category is the Machiavellian. They are master manipulators. They can be very lighthearted and easygoing in appearance, but they know exactly what they are doing. The Machiavellian is, in essence, very self-centered. The

Machiavellian is different from the Narcissist. The narcissists are just focused on themselves. The Machiavellian is more focused on how to use others to achieve their goals.

Another category is the Psychopaths. They are the people who are actually malevolent, and do indeed want to hurt others, or at least don't mind when they do. They are extremely callous, impulsive, and narcissistic. They like seeking out excitement and thrills, and if this negatively affects other people, they don't care. However, in the same vein as the first two categories, a Psychopath is able to be socially attractive, and they are good at making themselves seem charismatic and powerful.

The last category we will talk about is the Everyday Sadist. A Sadist has all of the characteristics of the first three types. However, they are not as manipulative as the Machiavellian, and they are not as interested in themselves as the Narcissists are. Rather, they are genuinely interested in cruelty, and they are actively looking for people to hurt. They might find people who want to be in toxic relationships because they are used to getting hurt. People who are sadists lean into these relationships because they know it will stay intact and toxic, and they can continue to reap the benefit.

Dark Psychology is all about knowing about these personality types and being able to handle them. Perhaps there is one of these types who is trying to affect your life in some way. Maybe you know someone who fits right into one of these categories. Maybe not, but it is probable that after learning about these types, you will start to analyze others around you and recognize some of them for who they really are. Most of us are subject to manipulation in some way, and we don't realize it. Dark Psychology is the study of this phenomenon, and it can help you to realize when you're being treated as an object or a means to an end.

Most people are good—right? Maybe you are the type of person who believes that most people aren't good. This is an argument that has gone on for centuries: the innate goodness, or lack thereof, in humans. Perhaps if we had a perfect society, there would be less impetus to be able to read and analyze people. However, even if everyone in the world were trustworthy and essentially good, that still wouldn't mean that it is not important to be able to analyze people. Wanting to be free from the danger of someone manipulating you is a good reason to want to be able to analyze people, but there are also other reasons.

Parents, for example, have to learn how to analyze behavior when they are raising children, for this allows them to read into their child's life and really get a sense of the wellbeing of their children. Therapists and other healthcare professionals need to analyze people in order to help them. Teachers need to be able to analyze people to assess where they are in their learning, in order to determine where they need to be. Even if you don't work in one of these professions, though, it is still important for you to be able to analyze people. Why? The short answer is that it makes life easier. It makes it easier for you to achieve what you want to achieve. It makes it easier for you to get through your day. It makes it easier to form lasting relationships and know which people to avoid.

It is important to be able to protect yourself. There are so many people in the world who fall prey to all sorts of scams and manipulation. We'd love to think that everyone in the world has great intentions, but that is not the case. The most vulnerable people in society tend to be scammed the most. Just think of the classic phone scammer situation. Phone scammers love to try and get in touch with older people, who are not as familiar with technology or might be out of touch with the processes of modern society. They make good targets to be manipulated because of this. People tend to see weakness and exploit it. The bad guys out there aren't looking for the toughest, sharpest people to exploit; rather, they are looking for the ones who will be easy.

This is the simple and brutal truth, and the way that you can help yourself and help others is by being more aware of people and being able to analyze people. When you are able to read into others' behavior, language, and body language, you can decode some of the messages that you are receiving, and you can learn more about people quickly. This may end up in many ways. Maybe you will be able to tell that they are good hearted and have only good intentions. Or, you might find that you are able to save yourself or someone else from a whole lot of inconvenience.

We all have a capacity for intuition. What is intuition? Well, it is a difficult thing to describe. It is a feeling, which we interpret into words, which comes from some part of our psyche. Intuition is a physical, emotional, and cognitive process that happens all at once, and it affects nearly every decision we make. Intuition is a very nebulous and esoteric concept. Intuition is something that comes from our core, and it has a lot to do with morality. It tells us what we think we should be doing deep down.

Intuition is very important for analyzing people. It can be thought of as the foundation for reading people. Information is important, and you can learn a lot about analyzing people from outside sources, but what it is going to come down to is learning to trust your intuition and really find a way to learn from yourself.

Communication is another part of why it is important to learn to analyze people. Communication is one of the most important skills that people will need to learn to function in this world. It is so important that people who can't learn to communicate often get shut out of society, even if it is unfair. When you are able to read and analyze people, all of a sudden some of the questions that you would've needed to ask before become unimportant. This is because you can already tell what is going on with the person before you start talking.

Analyzing people can give you the ability to predict what is going to happen and anticipate it, rather than having to wait and see. When you are not able to analyze people, you will find that you have to take more time to learn about people, and you don't have the immediate ability to see where problems and solutions are.

Analyzing people can also let you learn about yourself, and, indeed, learning about yourself will be a big part of the process in order to learn how to analyze others. Self-awareness is the skill of being able to see yourself objectively. This works in accordance with analyzing others. When you are able to analyze yourself and see patterns, it strengthens your ability to see patterns in others, and it helps you to develop a base of knowledge around behavior.

Finally, analyzing others can be seen as a spiritual pursuit. The pursuit of knowledge in this area is one of the most personalizing and emotional pursuits; when you learn to analyze people, you learn to be a better person. You start to think about your values, what you think is right and wrong, how you perceive others, and what you want to be.

Chapter 2: Body Language and Non verbal Communication

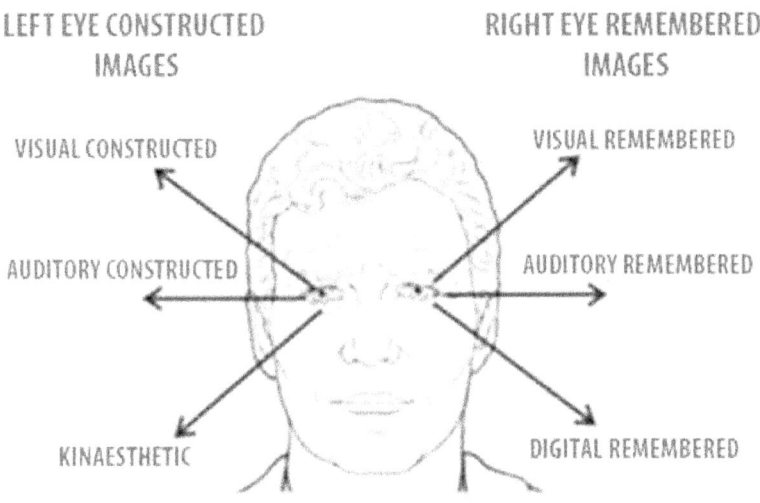

LEFT EYE CONSTRUCTED IMAGES

RIGHT EYE REMEMBERED IMAGES

VISUAL CONSTRUCTED

VISUAL REMEMBERED

AUDITORY CONSTRUCTED

AUDITORY REMEMBERED

KINAESTHETIC

DIGITAL REMEMBERED

Non-verbal communication is a huge part of your life, whether you realize it or not. Each time that you talk to a person, there are tons of messages that are being conveyed through the slightest body movements. When you experience this, you are just talking to the person, and you are listening to what the person is saying, and you are using your mind to connect with them. However, your visual, smell, hearing, and other senses perceive tons of information that is being processed automatically.

Language is a blunt force tool. What is language supposed to do? It is supposed to convey thoughts, ideas, concepts, and stories to other people accurately. It gives us a way to interact and puts us all on one level of communication so that we can make simple messages to each other and get by. However, language is also responsible for transmitting the most important and deep and abstract concepts. What it comes down to is the complexity of our everyday experience. How could you actually describe the flow when you're replaying basketball and making every shot? How could you really describe that in words to someone and have them actually know what you were experiencing? What about when you eat a piece of chocolate? Get broken up with? These are things that cannot be described in words, and yet we try to describe them. Sometimes it is done in ordinary conversation; sometimes, it is done in art or literature.

Language is what mutes and bottlenecks our experience into what we are able to convey to other people. Language is so limited in its ability to truly share our experience with others, and it is that limitedness that makes it, so that body language is so important. You are often experiencing both at them at the same time; you are experiencing someone's language simultaneously with their body language. Non-verbal communication is not all just body language, but a huge part of it is body language.

Think about one interaction that you have had in the last few days. It could be anything from buying something at the store or to a wedding—any tiny little interaction that you had. Try to imagine the interaction from the very beginning.

Body language is comprised mostly of a few factors: affect, posture, and motion. Effect refers to a person's facial expression. If a person is smiling, you could say that they have a bright effect. A person's effect is not always congruent with what they're saying and experiencing. You might see this in someone who is talking nervously about something, and they begin to smile. This means that their expression does not fit whatever they are talking about and that there is incongruence in their effect. When a person has a congruent affect, their facial expressions will change and be malleable. A person who has a congruent and secure affect will be expressing whatever they're thinking about or talking about on their face.

Posture is the way that a person holds himself or herself. This comes from their orientation to the world this can be found in the Enneagram of personality that we talked about earlier. These personality types describe basically an orientation to the world. Some people rear oriented as warriors, others are oriented as perfectionists. The way that a person's personality is will dictate the way they hold themselves physically. A person who is up in their mind will have the posture of a distracted person. A proud person will lead with their chest. What the chest symbolizes is a place of pride. It is where the heart and lungs are, and ties are protected by a cage of bones it is obviously a very important part of our bodies, and when we lead with that, we are showing that we are confident.

What would the chest be doing on a person who did not feel confident? If a person is not confident, they will be not is leading with the chest, rather it will be collapsing. Think about a person who is not confident, and how their shoulders move forward, and their posture seems tired or broken. They are the ones without confined because they are trying to protect their heart.

Another aspect of nonverbal communication is art. When we talk about art in this sense, we are talking about the capital "A" Art that includes sculpture, writing, acting, and all the creative arts. Even when language is involved, it is not verbal communication, it is writing. All of these fall under nonverbal communication. Learning to participate in artistic creation can help you to be a person who is more in touch with this part of communication.

Art can have all kinds of functions. Sometimes its function is to help sell things. This is a form of communication. When you hear something on the radio that is a catchy jingle that makes you feel a certain way about a product that is a deep form of communication. Art can help us to dance, to think, to feel joy or sadness, to help make things clearer, to make political action, to call to war, to call for peace. Music has a variety of functions. It can be used to help us energize or relax. Art is the same way.

Non-verbal communication is happening all the time; you are just not noticing it. Your gaze has a deep implication on how people perceive you the way you walk can tell people a whole lot. A person is a private person when they do not show you much with these.

Some people do not have the power of verbal communication. Some people are people who have very advanced dementia or other mental disorders such as advanced schizophrenia. Others could be people with learning or developmental disabilities like autism or Down syndrome. Can these people still communicate? Absolutely! They can communicate because their lives have revolved around learning ways for them to communicate.

Some ways that it might be easier to communicate with people who are non-verbal are touch, music, art, or hand symbols. People who are non-verbal tend to experience are in a deep way.

Some people have learning or developmental disabilities that prevent them from reading non-verbal cues. People with Autism Spectrum Disorder have a hard time deciphering the cues of behavior and non-verbal communication. ASD is a somewhat mysterious condition, and it is only diagnosed and marked by certain behavioral patterns and lack of social ability. This makes it a fascinating condition to learn how to help people with ASD to function better. In order for kids with ASD to be able to function better, they have to be helped to have integration. This means that they must learn to use their sensory inputs in concordance with their cognitive abilities to learn what a person is expressing. They will have to learn that when a person has their face all scrunched up, and they are yelping, that a person is angry. They have to learn about the body language of a sad person and how to act around that person.

This is pretty much what we are doing in this book, except we are talking about it on higher-level order. Rather than teaching kids how to learn the basic cues of non-verbal communication, we are trying to encourage you to learn to trust your intuition and be able to analyze behavior patterns on a deeper level.

This means that when you experience a behavior pattern, you are able to surmise what this means for you and what it means for other people around you. Instead of thinking about your feeling and worrying about it, you are able to either express it or act on it or do whatever wiles they need to do.

This is where the intuition comes in. you've got to trust what you are feeling about a person. If you see that a person walks into the room with a smile you've known before, and they act a certain way that you saw a person act, and you can know that they are trying to deceive you, this will make your life a little bit easier, as you can have that knowledge going in.

If you start to go to a new church, and at first you like it because of the community, but then you start to feel that it is just not the right place for you, this is intuition. We can use intuition to the behavior patterns of other can know if they will be good partners, good friends, etc.

Let's use the example of dating to try and illustrate what we are talking about when we talk about intuition. A new partner will be a new experience. It will be something that comes to you when you need it. People that we get involved with are generally on the same level of personal development as we are. If they aren't, these will inevitably lead to tension in the relationship. When we get into a romantic relationship with a person, we start to blend together our patterns of behavior. This means that you will seek out a person that will tend to increase the behaviors that you want to increase within yourself.

This is a good and bad thing. It is a natural process that lets us select people to get into relationships with so that we function better in our lives. However, if we are not able to see how we are not functioning well in our lives, then we will just be looking for someone to help us continue the patterns that we already find so easy to do. This is how patterns in relationships are perpetuated.

Chapter 3: Analyzing Others' Emotions

The way to learn how to analyze others' emotions is through the skilled ability to identify emotions. This may seem like an easy thing to do at first, but it may be very challenging for some people. Emotions are very subtle, and there is often more than one going on at once with a person.

Emotions are a physical state, that doesn't necessarily precipitate thought content, but often do. Sometimes an emotion will be experienced without words and will be expressed immediately. An example of this is a person feeling extremely angry, and in a split second, hitting someone else physically. We are not condoning this type of violence, but it is an example of a person reacting to emotion without thought content and expressing their emotion.

The other side of this would be a person who can't express their emotions and rather gets all up in their head with it. This often happens with people who are depressed or anxious. Anxiety tends to have big effects on thought patterns and thoughts; in this case, will often turn to negative self-talk or worry. Worry is a huge byproduct of anxiety, and they tend to go together.

Identifying emotions, then, is the study of seeing what's going on in the body. This can be well achieved by mindfulness, which we will talk about in more detail later. Mindfulness is a state of awareness of the body, which is helpful in being able to identify emotions.

When children get to the age of being able to express emotions and identify them, they often lack in the skill that it takes to be an adult and identify emotions. A child or an underdeveloped adult will not be able to describe their emotions naturally and accurately. They may mislabel certain situations, or they may not have the words to describe how they feel. A child may describe their experience as "mixed-up" when, in fact, they were angry. Sometimes people will mistake sadness for anxiety.

It takes a while to develop the skills to label and identify your emotions accurately. There are many ways to do this. The ones we will talk about in this chapter are journaling, self-reflection, and art.

Journaling is a great exercise for anyone looking to increase their emotional intelligence, because it involves externalizing your thoughts, getting them out into the world so that you can have a more objective experience with the material of your psyche.

Journaling about anything, even the most mundane subject can feel great and give you a sense of perspective on your day and what you want to do going forward. Journaling can be easy; it doesn't have to be difficult or seem like a punishment. Journaling is best started gently. You may want to buy a specific notebook for the purpose. Some people enjoy typing. Heck, if you want to get creative and experience a different tactile environment, you could buy a typewriter specifically for the purpose of journaling.

Do whatever you need to make it interesting and engaging for you. Start by writing down details from your day, and then start recording more and more detail. You can look into particular days when you have an emotional experience. First, try to isolate the emotional experience and describe it. Try to remember what was happening in your body, what was happening in your mind, and try to recreate the scenario in your head. Feeling what is happening in the body in these scenarios is a great way to elicit the emotional response in yourself so that you can monitor it and observe it.

Once you do this a few times, you can check your notes from each instance of emotional experience and see if your results are consistent. When you felt angry on Tuesday, the 11th, did you feel the same physical impulses in your body as to when you were angry the next month? What was the thought content of each emotional experience, and how did they match up? You might find some interesting data and information in here to gain awareness into how you experience emotions.

Each person will experience emotions differently, and this is good and necessary. Some people will cry when they feel sad; others will rage. Some people are comfortable with some emotions more than others. For example, someone might be comfortable being the angry person because this is where most of his or her experience lay. They have grown up around people who express their angry easily, and they themselves express anger easily. When it comes to sadness, however, they have no idea of how to express or show it. They may even be ashamed to show their sadness. Some demographic groups tend to lean one way or the other.

Another method to redevelop emotional awareness is self-reflection. Again, you should try to do this, however, is comfortable for you. If you like to be in nature, visit your favorite nature-filled place and have a moment in silence to think about a recent emotional state you have. You could also pay attention to your current emotional state, and ask yourself, "How am I feeling right now? Why am I feeling this way?" you can also explore the experiences that you had to lead up to your current emotional state, and from here, you can find strategies to increase or avoid those emotional states.

Yet another method is art. Art is a great way to use non-verbal expression to increase your mental well-being. Art is a magical carrier of emotion for humans; we tend to use art to understand the world and make sense of it. This is not the only function of art. However, there are many functions. One is dancing; others are relaxation, grief, mourning, celebration, and war rousing. There are many functions of music, and nearly all of them our emotions. Music is a great example of an art form that can transform the emotional experience and bring about emotional awareness.

Once you have the level of awareness that is required to identify emotions, you can use this knowledge to apply it to others. Take note of the process of the emotion that someone you are familiar with goes through. Once you have developed deeper levels of understanding around this, you can see it in other people. Then, from there, you can make decisions about how to act with a clear mind.

Once you have established the emotional state that someone is in, you can use that information to think about the best way to act. You have to take into account what their reaction will be along with your goals. Your goals for the situation sometimes will have to take a backseat, because a person just isn't able to deal at that moment.

Chapter 4: Tools and Skills

The first relevant skill that will be discussed here is neutral thinking. Neutral thinking is different because we tend to get wrapped up in all sorts of experiences and thoughts. Thinking objectively about ourselves may take some practice. When you learn to think objectively, you will be noticing what your thoughts, feelings, and behaviors are without being judgmental. Dark Psychology relies on you being able to separate from emotion. Emotions can lead to a distorted view of the world or in certain situations. Emotions cloud our judgment and our minds, and it doesn't allow us to be clear-headed.

In order to progress as a person, we must learn that we are not our thoughts. Your thoughts are not you. They don't represent you as a person. They are independent of you. Thoughts are not something that you try to have happen; they are automatic. You must just learn to ride the wave of your thoughts. This will require that you sit back, relax, and just watch your mind like a TV. See what is on the television as it flips through channels automatically. It will go from here to there, from yesterday to tomorrow. The mind will be all over the place, sort of offering different scenarios for you to think about, and you get to decide what you pay attention to. You can practice dealing with various thoughts by just seeing them come into your consciousness as if through a window, floating, and then coming back out of the window and leaving your consciousness.

This visualization can help you to realize that your thoughts are separate things from you and that they're floating out in the spheres, but they are not actually real. This is an outing that most people don't realize: those thoughts are not real.

If you take a minute to consider the complexity, you will realize that thoughts are an incredibly abstract concept. It is when we are using language that we had to learn, to spontaneously develop content, in our heads, using our voice, only to ourselves. It is something that you can definitely take time to trip out on if you'd like. Just take a while and the thing about the wonder of consciousness. Consciousness basically means human consciousness, not animal consciousness. The human version is something that is the most wondrous tool that we know of in the universe. The human mind is something that is so great and vast that it has created civilizations accounted for the force of incredible good and devastating evil. The minds not quantifiable at all—it only exists in the abstract. Certain methods can quantify behavior or brain chemicals or some parts of brain function, but the body can actually know what happens in the mind.

Just think about that: you can never actually know what another person is experiencing. They can describe it to you, but, as we will discuss, language is a blunt force tool, and may not always be accurate. All of the descriptions and quantification in the world cannot accent for this basic separation. It's a separation that makes us unman and drives the need for individualism.

The next major tool that we will discuss is listening skills. Developing listening skills is a very important tool for analyzing people. When we are talking about analyzing people, we are talking about the ability to understand others, and what better gift to have when trying to understand others than to listen to them? Listening skills give us a key into other people's lives, and to have that key is a responsibility as well as a privilege. You must treat others with respect and don't abuse the power that comes along with being a good listener.

A person who is a good listener can go through an entire conversation with minimally speaking or asking questions. They may be able to guide the conversation along shout saying anything at all, by suturing their body language. They might be so preoccupied in listening to the person that they don't feel the need to talk at all. Depending on whom mocha a person needs to talk about and how bad they need to talk about it, this can vary from person to person.

Developing listening skills can be the difference between being a poor communicator and a good communicator is able, to sum up all that the other person has said. A person who is good at communication will be a good listener because they know how to absorb the information with strength and attention to detail. Communication depend s on the interflowing words between two people there must be a circle-type feedback loop between two entities to develop strong communication.

Listening skills are when you feel a certain way about someone. Can you remember a time when you felt held, and loved? T might be a parent or s a schoolteacher or counselor, or someone else. That is what a really great listener can do. They can make you feel smart. They can make you feel like you are participating and angering with them in a fair and good level. People like to be seen and heard, and you can give people a surprising amount of validation by just paying attention to them.

Being able to do this for people, then, is an indispensable skill. Therapists have to learn down to do this, and they aver to learn how to be impartial observers to whatever is happening. When a person is listened to, they feel themselves in the world, and they feel its transformational powers.

In fact, many of the people who go to therapy for some other reason think they have some large need for therapy in one area realize that they just needed attention and love and to feel like they are listened to. People will go to therapy not realizing this, and session enfetter session if the therapist is a good one, they will find themselves feeling better just by having talked it out. Some people crave being listened to, and they never get it.

It is hard to ask for what you need, and sometimes it can help just to ask to be listened to. Sometimes you need to find someone who is a professional to help you along. Ultimately, in order to develop listening skills, you have to be a person who is interested in the world and interested in other people. You need to be a person who likes to find out why people do the things they do, and you most are a person who likes to bring joy to people.

Another important tool for self-awareness and analyzing others is journaling. Journaling is an excellent way to externalize thoughts and feelings. When you have experiences, those thoughts and feelings that are associated with experiences start to build inside you. You have a choice. You can express them or keep them repressed. The first choice is the better one because to keep repressed feelings in for so long is never sustainable. Repressed feelings find ways to leak out of the system in many other ways, whether it be unexpected aggression or acting out in other ways.

Journaling gives you a chance to say what you need to say out into the world. Some people will find this more difficult than others. Journaling gives you some distance between you and your thoughts, which is necessary because to be able to observe something, you must be outside of it. It's hard to give measurements of the fishbowl when you are a goldfish swimming around in it. Journaling makes our thoughts seem less crazy and less out there and gives us a chance to see what we what to be like. Some people will find that journaling freely is easy. Some won't.

Free-journaling is a great skill that you can learn to practice. At first, give yourself five or ten minutes to just write whatever comes out. Don't filter it—try not to stop. It doesn't have to be related to any one topic; you just need to let the words flow. This is incredibly challenging to do, honestly. It will be a fight to keep it up for longer than five minutes at first. However, writing is like a muscle and the longer that you flex it, the more you will be able to journal about your life successfully and easily.

Journaling is a great example of what analyzing people is all about: exploring, looking, investigating, trying to think critically about oneself, in the hope of ultimately understanding oneself to the degree that you can apply yourself in the world to the way that you desire. Emotional intelligence is both about being logical and having reason and science behind you, but it is also about the raw experience of experiencing everyday emotions and thoughts, from the very mundane to the deepest depths of human expression.

Journaling can be both. BF Skinner was a famous psychologist who came up with the concepts of behaviorism. Behaviorism is a strain of psychology that emphasizes looking at things in a measurable way. An example of a study in the style of behaviorism would be something like training a horse to run a lap for a carrot. Each time, the behavior is reinforced by the treat, in this case, a carrot; a nod the horse learns to run abroad the lap by itself a do the behavior for the reward. This type of psychology lets you treat everything like a science experiment, and this is a great way to get some empirical data on your problems

You can try to incorporate the principles of behaviorism into your journaling by taking data about yourself and analyzing it. If you want to go full-on scientific method, you can develop a hypothesis and test it. Your hypothesis may be something like "I will exercise more if I eat breakfast every day." Then, in your journal, record how many times in a week you exercise, and how many of those days you ate breakfast. From there, you can do further testing, learn your patterns of behavior, and get to where you want to be. This will make you feel like an amateur scientist, and that's' okay because it is good to be your own scientist sometimes.

Another important tool for analyzing people is mindfulness. This helps you tap into your intuition. Mindfulness is awareness, in the present moment, without judgment. Mindfulness is paying attention to whatever the object of the mindfulness is- this could be thoughts, it could be feelings, and it could be bodily sensations. Whatever the object of your attention is, you use that to practice focusing your mind for small periods of time, and then work up to larger amounts of time. Mindfulness ultimately refers to the integrated awareness of every experience in the woody, whether it is bodily sensations alone, or if there are other aspects of the experience that pop up. These could include smells, sights, or whatever else. The ultimate goal is to get to a place where your mindfulness captures your entire expertise at any moment. This will take lots and lots of work.

The way to start a mindfulness practice is to start by paying attention to the breath. The breath has several physical qualities. It may have a sound. It may just be detectable by feeling the bodily sensations in your chest and nostrils. It may have other qualities, other textures that you can pay attention to. It is also a rhythmic phenomenon, which makes it a great way to tune in to the body.

When you start, just take a second to get comfortable and find where you want to sit for a minute. When you have found a place to sit or lie down, then you can just start paying attention to your breathing and focus your attention all oven the breath. Each time you inhale, try to feel it in your nostrils or belly, and when you breathe out, try to feel it then as well. When you are doing this, your thoughts will come into your consciousness. This is okay and to be expected. When you experience thoughts, just let them go away. You can acknowledge that they exist, but when you can, just return your attention to the breath. This becomes a cycle of getting distracted and then coming back to the breath, and this is the way that you can start to develop a practice of paying attention to the body. Here is one exercise to try when you are starting out to number each breath, and when you breathe in, count 1. The exhale does not have to be counted. When you breathe in again, count 2; and then you just continue as far as you want, or you can start over when you get to ten. This will give you a way to connect to each breath and make sure you are paying attention to each and every moment that you are experiencing the breath.

This practice has a profound effect on the body. As you start to pay more attention to the body, you will find that you are able to be more present in your life. See, most of us have the problem of lending too much credence and too much importance to our thoughts. Our thoughts are not voluntary, they are just something that happens to our bodies and minds, and it is something that we just need to learn to cope with as human beings. It is not something that you should judge yourself for. People start to care a lot about their thoughts. This might take the form of worry when a person is always concerned about the future for the past. This might take the form of over-analysis, where a person is not able to just enjoy things without spending too much time thinking about it. It might lead to a person not being able to connect with other people, and being too much in their head when they should be with another person.

Mindfulness practice fights giant this imbalance and helps us to be individuals that are more integrated. It does this by helping to train you to learn to be a more in-the-body person than an in-the-head person. This will also lead to more emotional intelligence, where a person is able to tell more about their emotional experiences. The emotional experience is something that happens in the body. It is not a thought event, but rather a physical event. So, you can pay more attention to your emotional experience by paying attention to the body, and this will lead to a higher level of awareness.

You might ask how a higher level of awareness can lead to an increase in your ability to read people. Well, if you think about what it takes to read people, you will find that an awareness of self is important. It lets you know that when you feel angry with a person, you are actually angry and you can have more confidence in yourself that you are expressing the emotion that is what you want to express. You can trust your gut more when someone tells you something that might not be true. You can be more in touch with your experience with other people, and they will be able to trust you to be an authentic person. Just by being more authentic, you will be able to read people easier because it is something that draws other people out.

Chapter 5: The Art of Deception

Deception is constantly happening. You may or may not realize it. Since the birth of advertising in the '40s and '50s, we have been subjected to a large-scale invasion of manipulation. Advertising is a great lens through which to view Dark Psychology because many of its prime characteristics are utilized through advertising.

In the postwar era, America was very prosperous. Millions of Americans moved into a new house in the suburbs. They wanted to raise kids away from the struggles of urban life, where there existed crime and other unwanted phenomena. Most families at this point had a car, a kitchen stocked with the nicest appliances, and a big house with room for everyone. What else was part of the standard equipment for a family at this time? A TV. Families would gather around the TV and watch programs together. It is hard to imagine now the scarcity of "screens" that existed at this time. These days, we all have our own screens in our pockets, and we can pull them out and enjoy almost any media immediately. Back then, TV was a big deal.

With TV came commercials. NBC, ABC, and CBS reigned supreme, providing most of the programming for the entire nation. This was back when broadcasts were live, in black and white, and were only on for a couple of hours each night. Advertising started to incorporate messages about lifestyle. To be a fashionable American family, you needed to have certain things. A car was one, and a TV was another. There were certain possessions that started to become fashionable to have. Why were we buying that cookbook? It wasn't because of its functionality, or that a family member had passed it on down. It was because it was cool, modern, and fashionable to own that cookbook. Or that Ford. Or that Magnavox. All of a sudden, brand names became very important. This was not for any real reason; it was just because people wanted to sell those items.

Do you see where we are getting with this? This is an example of Dark Psychology. Advertising back in the 50s and 60s did not care about the quality of life of people who were buying the products. Rather, they were just concerned about making money. How can they make money? They decided to make money by manipulating the population. They decided that they could convince all of us, through their messaging, that their product was something that was necessary and important. They did this by selling the products as a part of an excellent life. No longer was functioning and surviving the goal. The new goal was to be glamorous.

This is what people who deceive do. They provide you with messaging. They sell you things. They sell your ideas. They tell you how things should be, and they start to convince you that there is no other way to be happy unless you buy a certain thing or place your support behind them. Sound familiar? You might be thinking of someone who does this already.

Now, this is still happening, and the psychology of advertising continues to this day. People are still influenced in manipulative ways from advertising. The strategies shift and change, but the essence is still there. One new phenomenon that has popped up in the last decade or so is the "ethical" component of selling. This is a strategy where someone is made to think that by buying a product, they are being ethical or helping someone else out somewhere in the world. An example of this is Starbucks Coffee. Starbucks successfully branded itself as a "fair trade" or ethical company. They went on campaigns to make it appear that they source their coffee from places that are more sustainable than the average coffee company is. They also have run countless promotions that purport to contribute to charities and other beneficial organizations. The most recent part of this is the reusable straw strategy. By calling attention to the environmental impacts of plastic straws, the company has encouraged people to buy permanent metal straws. Supposedly, with a metal straw, you are using it over and over, and therefore reduce your impact on landfills and other environmental problems. This, on the surface, will make people feel that they are "better" or "ethical" in their choice to buy a coffee from Starbucks. In reality, the impact made by reducing the use of plastic straws is so tiny that it barely makes any difference. The environment is not really benefitting from this situation. Who is? Starbucks. They are selling their product by telling you that buying their product is actually good for the environment. It is impossible to compare the difference in waste before and after people started using non-disposable straws because there hasn't been any change. The only change is that Starbucks gets a little bump in their sales because people think that they are "off the hook" for switching to non-disposable straws.

This is one modern conception of how we are deceived as consumers. The area of advertising is so rich for analysis in Dark Psychology because it is an area that has used the principles so successfully for such a long time. What might be more challenging is being able to analyze more personal relationships and how you are deceived. You can think of it on a large scale, but it might take some time to do a proper analysis of when these manipulation tactics are used on a smaller scale in your personal life.

The tactics are often the same. A person will tell you why you need to do something. The motive may be different. Sometimes a person will want to elicit a certain behavior from you under the guise of health. They may say that something is healthy for you, and that's why you should do it. Meanwhile, they are just encouraging you to do the "healthy" thing because they benefit from it. Another motive might be fashion or "coolness." This is how peer pressure works when you are a kid. Other kids suggest that in order to be cool or fashionable, you have to do certain things or be a part of certain things. The real reason they want you to do something is not that it will make you cool, but rather that it will make their life better in some way. Maybe they don't want to be alone, or maybe there are other reasons, but to be sure, peer pressure has been labeled for a reason.

There are specific body language devices that you can look out for when someone is trying to deceive you. Often times, a person who is lying or trying to deceive will change their head position quickly. This is something that a person does when they are not relaxed. When you are relaxed, your head will generally stay still and fluidly motioning with your neck. When someone is telling you something that they themselves don't believe, they might move around their head in a quick motion. This might appear as jerking or twitching. They might also have some sort of change in their breathing. This also has to do with relaxation. A person who is not being deceiving will not need to change their breathing, because again, they are relaxed. When a person is deceiving you, they will start breathing more heavily or more shallow.

Have you ever noticed the opposite of these signs, when a person is standing very still? A person standing very still can also be a sign that a person is being deceived because they are uncomfortable. Movement should be relaxed and generally unconscious.

Another sign is repetition. When you ask someone a question, and they take a while to answer it, they might start repeating the question or repeating their answer over and over. Repetition is their unconscious way of trying to convince you that they are telling the truth, when in fact, they are not. Repetition can be a nervous trait, but often times it is a sign that a person is not telling the truth.

People might have fidgety body movements when they are lying. One thing that people do when they are deceptive is covering their eyes or mouth. They may also just touch their mouth or other parts of the face. This goes along with another behavior that is common with lying: covering vulnerable body parts. This is a behavior that goes way back to our instinctive, animal roots. By covering important body parts, they are protecting themselves from physical attack. This is probably not something that they are thinking about doing; it is an unconscious act. Parts of the body that people might instinctively cover when they are lying might include the throat, chest, neck, head, or abdomen.

Have you ever noticed a person who was pointing a lot when they were speaking? This is also a sign of possible deception. Pointing is a subtle aggressive behavior. When you are pointing at something, you are directing attention to that thing. It could also be seen as singling someone out to draw him or her out into a vulnerable position.

There are also speaking mannerisms that people do when they are trying to deceive others. These speaking mannerisms include providing too much information or when it becomes difficult to speak. When someone tries to talk a lot to cover up their lie, they are hoping that you will be inundated with information that will overpower the strength of your intuition. Speaking a lot and trying to convey too much information betrays the deception in their words. On the other hand, some people might find it difficult to speak when they are lying. They might get a case of the dry-mouth, or they might purse their lips or bite their lips.

Chapter 6: Toxic Relationships

There are many kinds of toxic relationships. They happen for a lot of different reasons. There are many different kinds of relationship dynamics, which can be called toxic. There is no one kind of relationship that is toxic; rather, there are many kinds, and they are toxic for different reasons.

One common toxic relationship formula is the helper and the helpless. This is a relationship that people get into where one person just wants to "fix" or help the other. The "helper" is obsessed with doing this for people, and they are not able to have a sense of self or ever get help with their own issues. The "helpless" accept help but never quite get fully better. The helpless will remain in whatever problems they have because that is the role they are used to.

This is just one example of a relationship that is toxic. Something like this may not be easily diagnosed from an outside viewpoint. Some people keep the details of their relationships private, and nothing significantly toxic can be detected unless you are privy to the inner workings of the relationship.

There are many other types of toxic relationships, as well. There can be relationships based on anger. Some people need someone to get angry at in order to release tension. These people have not properly expressed emotions in the past. When a person gets used to not expressing emotions, their emotions build up over time and start to leak out in other ways. When couples get into a streak of fighting and making up, they are in this type of toxic relationship. What it takes to get out of this is insight. The person who has not expressed their emotions must learn how to start to express their emotions in a healthy way, rather than blowing up on the other person.

There can be relationships based on social status. This is common in both friendships and romantic relationships. It is extra common in this era of social media, where everyone wants to look cool and be the most fashionable or exciting. People will get into relationships with other people because of their social status. They might have many friends, a good job, or they might just be attractive. Social status may be a factor in relationships, but it cannot be the basis for relationships. There must be some other reason that people stay with friends or lovers with each other than looking cool. Those nights out on the town only stay exciting for a little while, and after that, these friends or lovers will start to realize that they don't actually y have any depth in the relationship.

There can be relationships based on substance abuse. This is another category that is part of both friendships and romantic relationships. Some people find drinking buddies, and their primary mode of being together involves getting drunk. This can often be related to going out and doing social things, or adventures, or it might just be hanging out at a friend's apartment. It is not toxic to just have a friend to go to the bar with. It becomes toxic when that is the only reason for the relationship. This also happens a lot with drug users because the experience of being addicted to drugs is isolating. So, what do you do when you are addicted to a drug and need to find someone to hang out with? You find someone who likes to do the same drugs as you. It makes perfect sense that these might become toxic relationships. It becomes toxic when it is more based on drugs than any other reason to spend time together.

There can be relationships based on envy and jealousy. This often happens with romantic relationships. A little bit of jealousy is okay. However, many people start to get into a toxic situation where they are always looking out for the other person to cheat on them, and they use it as an excuse to cheat on the other person. What this boils down to is the person being too scared to break up with a person and to be alone. However, by staying in a toxic relationship, they are just perpetuating the hurt that it will cause.

There is also a relationship scheme known as codependency. Codependency is a somewhat nebulous term. It is sometimes known as a situation where two people are dependent on being together rather than being alone. Now, this is a complicated matter because humans are social animals, and we require relationships to have full and healthy lives. It makes sense that a person without friends or a romantic partner might feel lonely. This is to be expected. However, there comes a time when people become too dependent on one another and are not able to function outside of the relationship. Healthy relationships require differentiation of self. Differentiation is how much you are able to stand on your own in the world, and it is how you see yourself. A fully differentiated person is able to have confidence in their own ideas and views, and they are able to achieve results independently from other people. People who don't learn how to be differentiated will find themselves always looking for a person to glom onto.

This is where codependency happens. When a person is not sufficiently differentiated from their family or other systems, they start to lose their sense of self. This can cause people to have a lack of self-esteem and a loss of confidence. A person must be able to tolerate long periods of being alone in order to be able to be in a healthy relationship.

Many people do not realize this: that part of being able to be close to another person requires you to be able to be alone and be okay with being alone. Some people take to this quite easily and are good at being alone for extended periods. Some people hate it and get very lonely and anxious when they need to spend lots of time on their own. Some people get very anxious when they need to face a new situation that is unknown to them without someone to be with.

Understanding personality is a great way to be able to analyze relationships for toxicity. One way to do this is to study systems of personality. Many personality systems have been redeveloped in the history of human study. Throughout time, people have engaged in self-reflexive exercises to explore what it means to be a human and why we are the way we are.

One of these folks who were studying what it meant to be a man was Carl Jung. Jung did a lot of writing and research on archetypes. Archetypes are relatable things that we all see in life. See, Jung thought that since we all had common experiences -the sun, the moon, the dark of night and the light of day, and that this connects us with a collective unconscious. Humans have universal experiences, like birth and death, and love and heartbreak, and that these universal themes suggestive a psychic pre-ordained order in our minds. This is the idea that since we are all in human bodies experiencing the earth, there must be a commonality in our experience. These archetypes might manifest themselves in different ways in different cultures, but they are deeply held within us.

Since we are all connected to our physical experience and the earth in a very intimate way, there are forms of ways of living and personality that have come out into the consciousness as recognizable ways that people are the way that they are. The shadow is a symbol of the unconscious, and it is an analogy for a person's dark side, in the eyes of Jung. The shadow self-mirrors Freud's Id and is the animal side to our consciousness. It is what makes us fully human, and it is the place that we go when we are feeling animalistic in any direction, i.e., satisfying a need to have sex, eat, or protect oneself.

Jung's work has been processed over and over again and has influenced many spheres of thinking, including popular psychology and scientific psychology. The Enneagram system is a system of personality that may have ties to Jung's work, as many of the principles that he looked at are found there. The Enneagram has its roots in the Sufi tradition, and it was refined over the years by various thinkers. The Enneagram of personality loosely aligns with Jung's idea of personality, and it presents nine personalities as ways that we can recognize people behaving in the world.

The Enneagram is not a magic scroll that will tell the future and tell you exactly how a person will act in any given situation. Rather, it is a way that you can think about personality and a way for you categorize people into behavioral patterns and tell why they are the way they are and why they do the things that they do. It is not something that is crystal clear in every case. A person who you see one day might act a certain way because they are feeling a certain way, but then the next day they will act completely different. This does not discredit the Enneagram, for, in fact, the Enneagram is one the closest things to describe the indescribable. Like Jung's stereotypes, these personality types can be deeply tied to literature, movies, etc., and we tend to see them over and over and over in art and literature.

The first personality type in the Enneagram of personality is The Perfectionist. The Perfectionist is driven by a moral drive. They are good people, and this is because they grow up wanting to be good people. The Perfectionist will often have pathology relating to perfectionism. If a Perfectionist is driven in childhood always to be achieving and always trying to be the best, they can often grow up with habits that relate to perfectionism that will become problems later in life. The Perfectionist wants everything not only to be working in good condition, but they also want things to be moral. They see the world in good and bad, and they definitely want to be on the good side of things.

The Perfectionist will need to learn to calm down their perfectionist urges to reach self-realization. Self-realization is eating concept of people being able to be fully themselves and reach the potential theta they have in several different domains. These domains include but are not limited to leave, work, relationships, art, and whatever else a person needs to function. When a Perfectionist is able to realize that not everything needs to be perfect and that they can just reaccept what is going on around them, then they will be able to make more connections with other people and with themselves, and they will find that they have an easier time in life.

The second personality in the Enneagram is The Helper. The Helper wants to help people out, and they want the world to be a better place. The Helper will often find a helping profession, where they are working with another bole to help them in their lives. They height have jobs like doctors, therapists, nurses, physical therapists, etc. These people have a deep drive to help and be helpful. They want to give and be generous with themselves, and they expect other people to do the same. The Helper often gets into codependent relationships, where they want to help another person and they need the other person to need them. This can become an unhealthy dynamic, as the Helper is always looking for their next person to help even though the person will likely never change.

The helper must transition from this pattern if they want to engage in the practice that will lead to self-realization. A helper must realize that others can be helped, and they fill this role very well, but they must also acknowledge that they themselves need help nod they must learn to help them and accept help from others. When the Helper does this, they will learn that the world is not a bad and scary place and that they can actually be I the world and be helped by others, and that this will provide them with a sense of contentment. It is all about balancing your traits with the rest of your consciousness.

The third personality type in the Enneagram is the Achiever. The Achiever is a very optimistic and charismatic person. They like to go to the top of a mountain because they felt like it. Alternatively, they might have seen someone else go partway up the mountain, and they want to prove that they can achieve something greater than someone else around them can. Achieving provides a way for this person to find personal growth and feel good about them. This is a brood wee to position a psychic without the perfectionism; however, the achiever will eventually realize that achieving I only one dimension of human life. Achieving is something that we do when we need to move society forward, and it is essential that we have achieved in the world. However, the Achiever will have to learn about other aspects of human life, including loving, resting, taking care of others, and reflection.

Once an Achiever is able to do this, they will learn that achievement is not needed for them to win the love of tether's they can have love just the way they are. Acceptance is going to Abe a big task for the Achiever as they go on in life and try to make deep connections with other people.

The next personality described in the Enneagram is Romantic. The Romantic is driven by a deep need to make life meaningful, and they do it well. The Romantic loves oceans, fires, parties, sunsets, storytelling, drinks, coffee shops, bookstores, and the like. They want to live in one beautify moment forever. They want everything to be beautiful, and they enjoy the melancholy of life. They like to revel in the sadness fought life is, and they think of the human condition as a beautiful thing. The world rather is out on the road performing with a band than working in an office. They like to get lost in books and poetry, and they are usually good at conversation with others. The Romantic is oftentimes an artist, and they will often try to live as a musician, artist, actor, or radio host. They are people who are creative and spontaneous. One dark side of the Romantic is that they are prone to depression. This is because they feel so much in the world, and they are escapists because the world overwhelms them. They may not be very good at modulating their emptiness nod getting out of a certain mood state. They might feel that the world is too sad and dangerous for them, and this will often keep them in a depression.

In order to find self-realization, a Romantic will have to learn that not every moment in every day is beautiful. This will be where they need to find acceptance: not every day is beautiful, not every moment is a good moment. There are dry, humdrum moments that take up the better part of each day, and they will need to learn to cope with that. The Romantic will often be able to temper their earlier instincts for chaos and rebellion and find peace. They do this thought, acknowledging that the world is not always beautiful, but she is nothing they can do about that.

The next personality type on the Enneagram is the Investigator. The Investigator is driven by a need to perceive the world. They may web writers or journalists or scientists. They like to organize themselves in the world like a sponge, somebody who is always receiving information from the world. They believe that by observing and investigating, they will find truth and meaning. They are driven by the need to perceive. The need to perceive is something that we all have within us, but the Investigator is obsessed with it. They might suffer from a lack of personality in the self because they're a lays focus used on tethers and other systems and bodies to be convened with, then to investigate them.

In order to achieve self-realization, the investigator Weill need to learn how to turn that investigating light upon themselves and have space for self-reflection. The Instigator could be aligned with many different worldviews, but this doesn't change their core need to balance their urges. This will take the Investigator to have some sort of life-altering experience where they feel humbled. Only then will Whyte be able to shine a light on their closet in their mind and really learn what is up with them and how they can live in the world and thrive.

The next category of personality in the Enneagram is the Loyalist. The Loyalist wants to mother more in the world than friends. They don't like the physical intimacy of intimate relationships at first, and they are not so convened with family bonds. What they want are friends to surround them at all times and for them to have a full social circle with lots of different types of friends. The Loyalist will often have a group, or they might just have a one really good friend that they have found a symbiotic relationship with. They will find a person that they are able to accompany in the world and be loyal to, and the person who they are with will find ways to be a person that the person can be lay to. The Loyalist really dislikes conflict, and they will stave to avoid conflict at all costs. The Loyalist tends to get into a codependent relationship. Often times the Helper and the Loyalist will get into a codependent relationship weir the Helper wants to help the Loyalist change, but the loyalist is not interested in changing, but rather in prolonging the relationship. They will find themselves giving a little of what their other wanes at different times, and they will find that they are locked into relationships that are unhealthy and are really bad for them.

What the Loyalist needs to develop to reach self-realization is a sense of self and identity. They're so focused on themselves in the context of tethers, Althea the Loyalist will need to learn how to say what they want to see when they want to say it, and they will have to learn to be themselves around other people. Often times a loyalist will feel like the world has cheated them, that they were a good person and friend at theta they were not given in the same opportunity back to prove that they are the best. They will feel downtrodden and disappointed in the world, and they will need to take this feeling and learn to modulate it so that they are not feeling tile they're the only person in the world who is feeling that way. The Loyalist often feels that the world has some crazy order to it that they can't figure out. The Loyalist will need t to learn that that is not the case; actually, the world is similarly indeterminable to all people.

The Optimist is the social butterfly. This is a personality type from the Enneagram that loves to be with other people and loves to lift other people up. They are able to see the good in every situation, and they have fantastical drams about what old be in the future. The Optimist will be able to imagine realities that are not accessible to the everyday thinker, and they will vet driven by the need to fix, to achieve, and to bring people together. The optimist may be less of an achiever hand other, but hey have achievements in certain areas. The optimist loves to be able to light up a room and make people e laugh, and they want to see everyone around them grow to their full potential. The optimist loves eating new people, and they love being around children. The shank that life should be carefree and easy they want everything to be a good time, and they want everyone to be partying all the time.

In order to reach self-actualization, the optimist will have to realize that the worlds are a somewhat pessimistic place, and they will have to get more in touch with their feelings of sadness and fief. This happens slowly unless omen kind of dramatic even happens to cause an ego death in the person.

The next personality in the Enneagram system is the Protector. The Protector learned early on that this is a way they can control their environment: their own, sometimes physical, forces. They are good at helping other people out, but not in the same way as the Helper. They like to use butter strength to defeat their enemies and accomplish their goals. They are really good at sports, often, and they tend to be people who emphasize the physical form more than others do. They see the physical form as a metaphor for the mind, and where the mind goes, the body will follow. They see themselves as a having a role in the universe to tend to and take care of, to in an emotional sense, but more in the sense of watching out over a flock.

The Protector will need to realize a few things in order to reach their potential as human beading. They will need to learn that they, like everyone else, have weaknesses, even physical ones and they will learn to live with these deficiencies by earning to depend on other people. This will be hard for the Protector, as they really dislike exposing themselves to others, and they hate being vulnerable. The Protector is a person who will need to learn to embrace the inner child, and rather than telling them that they need to fight to survive, they will need to tell the inner child that it okay to cry, it is okay to be weak, it is okay to depend on others.

The final personality type that is presented by the Enneagram of personality is the Peacemaker. The Peacemaker is interested in harmony, and they like to be connected with other people nod they like to see this thrive in the community. The Peacemaker is driven by a moral compass, but not in a pathological way like the

Perfectionist. Where the Perfectionism wants everything to be perfect because it is good, the Peacemaker was everything to be good because pall will experience less suffering that way. There is always a pain, but the Peacemaker knows that there are pain and offers. One of them, pain, is never going to leave our lives. There will be aspects of pain, whether it is physical or emotional, throughout our lives. It is not something that we can escape. Suffering, however, is something that happens when he tries to deal with pain and can't really dale with it all the way. Then we are suffering. Ties are a state where we are fighting against being human, and it is the opposite of acceptance. The Peacemaker intuitively knows this situation, and they understand the dynamics of throw this works. They want to make the world a better place.

In order to make peace with the world for them, the Peacemaker must actually go the other way and learn how to be more of a fighter. This is the mistake that this personality type often faces: they don't realize that to enact the change that they would like to see in the world, they have to go out and do it. They may be meek or weak people in presentation, and they like to keep themselves out of battles. They need to be more like the Protector if they want to establish higher-level orders of consciousness. The Peacemaker knows when they are doing this. They must be able to learn how to stand up for themselves as well as others and to be assertive and fight the good fight.

The way that these personality types are situated in the Enneagram has significance, as well. There are triads and wings in the Enneagram system. These can be studied more if you are interested in the subject. The personality types presented here and other systems of personality basically give u a way to look at people and analyze their behavior. They can show us the way that people act in certain stations. They tell us about the innate drives of a person rather than just the venerable characteristics.

You must be careful in trying to apply the knowledge of personality types to your everyday life, and know that people might be tricky and may not be so easily figured out. On one day of the week, a person may be acting like a certain personality, and on another day, they might be acting like they are in a big mood that differs from the other day. Depending on whoever they want to be at the moment, something different is to be expected. However, there are certain ways that we orient ourselves in the world, and these contribute to our behavior. The personality types can tell you how to observe these and what to look for. There are many other systems of personality, which can open your perspective even more.

Personality is something that is not set in stone, but it does tend to be a way that a person functions not the world for most of their time. People can shift, however, and change in their lives. A person may have to actually make the shift from fitting in with one personality to an entire another personality type in their lifetime. It is not common, but it does happen. There are ways that you can derive some meaning from the personality types listed in the Enneagram, and they can be a good way for you to read people.

By being able to identify a perfectionist, for instance, you can then know why a person does what they do. When you realize that they might fit in well with the perfectionist personality type, then you can start to know that they want everything to be good and moral, and that is their highest motivation in life. Then you can adjust your expectations accordingly.

A big part of what the Enneagram allows for is for youth are able to adjust your expectations of a person. Many people think about everyone as having the same characteristics as them. Some people may have similar patterns and characteristics as you, but many do not. Expectations allow for you to be able to know what a person will be vale to handle, what a person will bearable to do in certain situations, and how much you can depend on them.

There are different thresholds that we all have in different areas. One of them is the discomfort threshold. Many people have high discomfort thresholds, and they're able to withstand certain types of pain better and longer than others are. Some people have high emotional pain tolerances and low physical pain tolerances. Other people will have the opposite experience: physical pain will be easy for them to endure, but the emotional pain of vulnerability will be difficult.

Intuition is an abstract concept. There is no way to study it, except to ask someone to describe his or her experience of intuition. Intuition is a combination of your spiritual self, your physical self, and your cognitive self all coming together. It takes into account the feelings that you are experiencing, the thoughts, and the bodily sensations that you are experiencing, and it tells you what feels right at the moment.

Intuition is a deeply human thing that is not explained easily. It isn't anxiety, it isn't a fear, and it is not an emotion. Rather, it is a combination of emotion, thought, and sensation that leads you to be able to make decisions. When you are feeling your intuition, try to follow it. Some people don't know what it feels like to be able to follow their intuition; they might not even be aware when they are getting the hint about something or somebody.

Intuition is that little feeling that this person is lying to you or that slight drop in the gut when you realize that you've won a prize. It is your body reacting before your mind can. The body's really an intelligent construction; we like to think of the minds the source of intelligence in the west, but that's only partially the case. The body is to thank for some of our peer feeling and intuitive processes, and the body is what tells us when we are in danger when we are being lied to, when a person needs genuine help, or when we are in love. A mind is a place that is filled with tight thoughts and ideas. The body is filled with actual sense data that is more trustable than thoughts.

Think about the last dream that you had. Were you aware that it was a dream? Probably not. There are some people who have reported that they are able to control their dreams, in a process called lucid dreaming. In this process, a person is able to point out to their sleep consciousness than they are experiencing a dream, and that what they are imagining is not actually real. When they are able to do this, people can then direct their actions in the dream. They can start to be more in control, and they can find a way to be in aware in their dreams.

Most people do not have this skill, however, which is perfectly normal. To them, it seems like their dreams are completely real. When they are experiencing dreams, they are not able to distinguish from reality, and even though that content of the dream may be fantastical and unrealistic, they find themselves believing that everything in the dream is true and is actually happening.

This just shows how unreliable our minds are. If they are able to construct a completely new reality where you can fly or do other, things that are completely unrealistic, then just imagine how far off you can get in your thinking in everyday life.

The body is not so fallible. The body doesn't think—it just reacts. The body is a place where you cannot control what is happening, and that is where the truth comes in. The truth is in body language because the body just reacts. There is no cognitive filter process.

When you feel a certain way about a person in your intuition, just try to see that that is valid. It may not be something that you want to act on, but you can start to realize that your bodily feelings of intuition are valid, and then you can start to do something with them. Many people grow up learning to ignore their intuition for various reasons. One such reason is that they were encouraged not to express emotions when they were younger. Many younger people with strict parents are like this; they are shown or told then they are kids that expressing emotions makes them weak and that they should not express emotions for fear of being abandoned or criticized. This is a very damaging way to grow up, and it affects a person's ability to be able to trust their intuition. For a person like this, confidence will be the key to developing the ability to trust the intuition.

This is a person with low self-esteem. A person with low self-esteem will have trouble trusting their instruction because they have either learned or told themselves that their gut is not something to be trusted. This is not the case, because, for everyone, his or her inner feelings are valid. So, this person will have to learn confidence. Exposure therapy is good for this; the principles of exposure therapy state that when you are exposed to something that you are uncomfortable with for an extended period of time, you will start to learn how to deal with it more, and you will start to be able to withstand periods of exposure to the stimuli more because you are able to take the heat, so to speak. This means that people with confidence issues should look to put themselves in places outside of their comfort zone. To start, you can try to put yourself in a position to take small risks. If a person has social anxiety, they could try to get a job in a coffee shop or somewhere where they will have to interact with a lot of people but on a limited level. This will get you thinking about how you can interact with people, and it will start to get you more comfortable with exposure to people every day. The more people that you interact with, the more you will start to learn that you are a cool and interesting person if you engage in good faith, and confidence will grow from there.

Confidence is what lets you do what you should do. Then that little feeling tells you that you should offer this person a job, or walk out of another situation, or drive a different route home, and you do it because you are confident in yourself and you have seen yourself succeed over and over. This is something that will need to take a little time, and yours is patient and kind to yourself through this experience.

There is no way to record intuition; there is no way to quantify it. This is something in your soul. It is something that might take some soul-searching to do. This is something that some people feel come from your ancestor, and there is a sort of collective unisons that we are all participating in together.
The idea of the collective unconscious is that we are all human beings and can relate to each other one human level. This means that our intuition will often match. Not always, but it is something that we can connect to with people who are in similar situations to us.

This is something that lies simmering below the surface of our minds and not so much on the surface. The intuition is a feeling, and it comes first before the thoughts. Thoughts are not so important. They might help you to understand your intuition, but hour thoughts are not your intrusion, they're an automatic process that is distracting you grow whatever bodily expiring you are having.

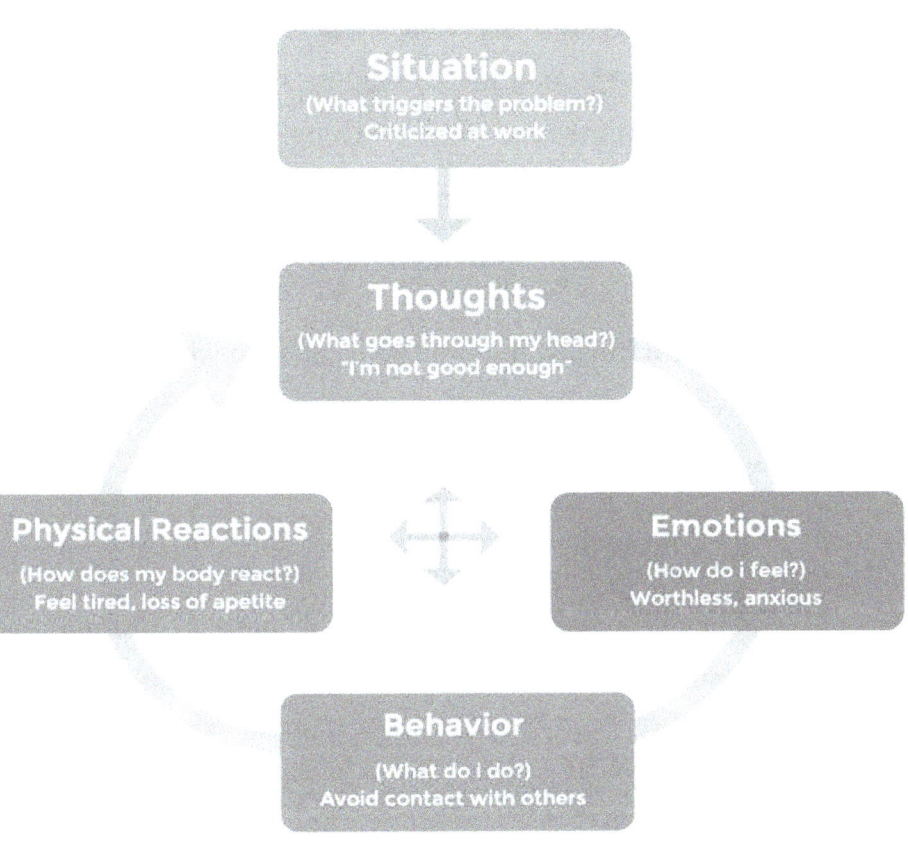

It can be very difficult to understand why people do the things they do. They might be driven by unconscious drives, or they might be hiding their behavior form the world. It is always impossible to know what a person is doing behind the scenes.

This is why it is very important to stick to what is observable about a person's behavior. If a person is usually about five minutes late, you can know that this is a part of their behavioral patterns, and unless something changes, they will continue always to be five minutes late to everything. At this point, you should not try to change the person's behavior, but rather accept it. If their being five minutes late is causing problems, then that is another story. If a person has a habit like this, and it begins to provide others with inconvenience, then a change will have to be made. However, most of the time, you can observe patterns of behavior like this and just let them be.

What does it take to change a person's behavior? Well, in this case, you can just remind the person that they have committed to being somewhere at a certain time, and that they should respect the boundaries of their work item and be there for when it starts. This is if you are responsible for the person's behavior.

If you are not responsible for working with a person, or otherwise have no reason to try to change the behavior, then all patterns must be accepted. This is hard for some people. Some people want everything to work out and be good for them, and they don't know who to accept the world around them.

Acceptance is key here. Accepting behaviors means that you don't judge whatever a person is doing. You can know that their behavior is self-destructive or bad for others, but this doesn't mean that you can't accept their behavior. Acceptance does not mean condoning. What it does mean is that you realize the extent to which you can affect someone else's behavior, and it is really looking at the patterns, which are observable and drawing conclusions from there.

Patterns are observable only in one way to us. It is important not to make assumptions about a person based on their observable behavior patterns. Patterns are merely the data that you have about a person. For example, a person might drink a cup of coffee every morning. Let talk about how much we can surmise just from this one single behavior pattern. One is the aspect of addiction. We can know that this person, judging from this one behavioral trait, has the capacity to be addicted to something. Pretty much all of us do. You cannot, for example, judge that this person is an addict and can't keep themselves from doing this. But a cup of coffee in the morning is an addiction.

Patterns can give your insight into the motivations of a person. If Sarah usually ends up having out with Mark rather than Jessica, this could be from multiple factors. It could be that Mark is a love attraction for her and that her drive to be in a romantic relationship is more important to her right now than her drive for friendships.

Concentration and attention are important skills to have when you are learning to read people. Your attention and concentration must be firmly affixed to one person in order to read them effectively.

People can be read because people's lives are a story. People go thought individualistic things that make them unique and themselves. Each person has a life story with many chapters, and each person contains multitudes. It is not a question of if you are able to read people, because people will show themselves to you. It is the question of if you will be able to read them and use that knowledge for your own good.

When you are trying to read another person, try to focus all of your attention on them, but still while observing them in a neutral way. Check out their posture. Are they standing up straight? Are they crouched or leaning to one side? This can tell you about the physical state of their body. Older people often lean into their posture and will be a bit more hunched over. This is a sign of age. Sitting up straight is a signal that a person is relatively healthy and young.

When people walk, they tend to lead with a certain part of the body. Some people lead with their heads, some lead itch their feet, some lead with the chest. This can give you great insight into the person's drives and how they conduct themselves. A person who leads with the chest may be proud and strong, and they like their physical appearance. If a man has shrugged shoulders that hang down and leads more with the waist, this gives you the idea that they are carefree and laid back. If a woman leads with her hips, it means that she is feeling confident. There are all kinds of ways that body language can give your insight into a person's personality.

One of them is how touchy or physically affectionate a person is. Some people like to have hugs the entire life, and they life to connect physically on a basic level in everyday life and conversation. Other people are not so comfortable with physical contact and prefer to eschew hugs for handshakes and a nod of the head. Neither of these is correct, as there is no correct approach to this. You just have to be cognizant of the boundaries that exist, i.e., not hugging a person who clearly doesn't want the physical contact.

The next main point to consider when you are reading people is the effect. What do we mean by effect? The effect is the way that the face is expressing thoughts and feelings. A normal effect is considered one that has a wide range of expression, for example, smiling when one is happy and having facial expressions that match what one is saying and doing. The effect is a big clue to how someone is feeling. People with some mental illness, for example, have flat affects. This means that their effect does not change very much when they say different things, and they're not able to express feelings with their faces. This comes with a variety of conditions. However, much less severe cases of restricted affect can come simply from being shy, anxious, or sad. A person may restrict their effect when they have social anxiety, for example. A person's thoughts can be wildly swinging all over the place, and their face is displaying a neutral, calm reaction. This can be a protective mechanism for some people, for when you hide your emotions; you and other people don't have to deal with the messy reality of where your emotions are. Some people display all of their feelings their face. When speed-reading people, you just have to determine who much a person's effect is actually representing their feelings. Then, you can engage.

Eye contact is a huge part of this. How much eye contact is the person making? Is it sustained and intimate? Is it broken up? Sometimes, people can be aggressive with eye contact, and it can actually be a way for people to act out their dominance in a situation.

Eye contact is a proximal thing that can connect and divide people. The term Male gaze" was coined to describe the interaction in eye contact or gaze alone. The male gaze is what it is because of the power of the eye. It is something that we often forget, but eye contact is a powerful tool when you make eye contact with someone, you are making a connection. This connection might frighten some people, and people who are shy or have problems with self-esteem will often avoid eye contact to a high degree. This eye contact is causing this a primal level of connection that they do not trust because they don't trust themselves, and they don't have confidence. A person with confidence is able to make eye contact with anyone they encounter and engage with them. People might be intimidating, but you can always engage with someone in good faith and have confidence in yourself to represent yourself and your ideas effectively.

The only way to start reading people is by practicing. You can give yourself some practice by intentionally putting yourself in a situation where you will be around other people and trying to observe them. Observe their tiny movements, try to see how they hold themselves by looking into their eyes. Do not try to linger, just try to make the interaction as normal as possible, with observing as much as you can about the person.

When you get home, write about it. Try to recreate whatever you saw and observed in the person and try to get every little detail known onto the paper. Try to describe what you saw in that person's emotional state, their effect, their smile or lack thereof, their body language, what words they used, and everything else.

Chapter 8: Machiavellianism

Machiavellianism is a set of traits that are centered on making plans, delaying gratification, and manipulativeness. The term "Machiavellianism" comes from the name of Niccolò Machiavelli, who was an Italian politician, philosopher, and humanist. Machiavelli wrote a great many works, and wrote in several domains, creating poetry, comedies, and songs. He also wrote about the unscrupulous behavior of politicians in his book The Prince. This is where he described behavior that seems terrible; he normalizes it by describing it as something that is effective and expected in politics.

Machiavelli goes against the norms of morality. He would be likely to describe something to be okay if it causes negative outcomes if the ultimate end was justified. Machiavelli thought that the end justified the means. Therefore, he was not one to worry about hurting feelings. He was more concerned with getting stuff done.

Machiavellianism is all about being self-centered. This is something that you might find you need to adjust in some way. It is not about being needlessly self-centered; it is more about being focused on individuality and achieving goals. Some people are too selfish in some ways. These people do not have goals and don't strive to make themselves better in some way. They are more interested in resting on their laurels and keeping their riches to themselves. In this case, a reduction of selfishness is necessary. Many people, on the other hand, need to increase their selfishness.

We are often told when we are younger that selfishness is inherently a vice. Sharing and kindness are rightly emphasized when we are growing up. However, selfishness is not such a black-and-white issue of morality, like some other issues. Selfishness is complex. If you are able to work for yourself and work towards a goal that will allow you to become what you need to be and, in that process, help other people or reach some other accomplishment, then you have facilitated a transformation that required selfishness. After all, we have subjective consciousnesses, which can't be fully shared with any other human.

Selfishness, when used to acquire certain goals, can be fully moral and good. Selfishness can allow you to focus on what really matters. It can allow you to become more fully self-realized.

The dark side of Machiavellianism is when it leaks over into unadulterated cruelty. The honorable side of Machiavellianism uses power to leverage itself into greater situations for the advancement of humankind, in one way or another. The dark side, on the other hand, replaces these goals with no goals at all. Many nihilists could be considered very Machiavellianism.

Remember those cartoons from way back in the day, which illustrated a demon on one shoulder and an angel on the other? This concept illustrates the idea of inner voices. We all have various inner voices that tell us to do different things. Sometimes the voice may be one of our consciences, and it tells us to do well and take care of others and ourselves. It might be a guilty voice, which tells you that you have done wrong that needs righting. There are myriad of inner voices that we have. In Machiavellianism, the voice is always asking one thing: "What will be best to dominate this situation and achieve my goals?"

This voice might be interrupted by other voices, who might tell you things like "You're not good enough to succeed" or "That's enough for one day" or many other things. Part of utilizing the concepts of Dark Psychology for yourself is learning to single out the voice you want to listen to. Sometimes, the voice telling you to call it a night might be correct. Other times, though, it is wholly appropriate to listen to the Machiavellianism voice.

You could also think of it as a spirit. The spirit of this principle is the spirit of self-preservation, dominance, success, and excellence. It is sometimes ruthless. Machiavellianism is centered on achieving the highest highs of potential that is within you. Think about the things that have kept you from achieving your goals in the past. They might have had something to do with self-esteem. Maybe you weren't equipped for the task at hand, and you had no choice but to accept defeat. Maybe you were too lazy. Maybe you didn't work hard enough.

These are the things that you will be able to avoid if you try to center your achievements towards Machiavellianism. It is all about forgetting these setbacks and pushing ahead. When you are in this successful mindset, these other concerns don't even bother you. When you're in this mindset, everything else floats away. It all becomes about what you need and what you want. You don't have control over other people in the world. All you have control over is yourself. What gets in the way of that control? Emotions and desires.

Emotions and desires are the root of laziness and letting yourself go. You must be able to detach yourself from emotions and desire. Emotions will distract from your ultimate goal. Desires must be culled down to just the very most important ones. Let go of these frivolous distractions.

One thing that a Machiavellian worth his or her salt can do is analyze people. When you are looking to read people, you must understand their context. What does this mean? It means knowing the when, where, how, and why they are in the world.

Our cultural upbringing and our family of origin shape us all. The culture that we grow up in has a great effect on our values, our career trajectory, and other realms of if development.

If we take the USA as an example of a culture, we can identify certain aspects of it that affect how we are the way we are. In the USA, we tend to be pretty focused on making money. The entire structure the government is set up to be for the people, but much of it has been corrupted by the purposes of making money. Capitalism is what we strive to live under, but it is a certain kind of capitalism, one that forces us to go to college, choose a job, and live a predetermined path. The reason for this is productivity.

Think about a life where productivity isn't the goal. What would you do? Maybe you would spend more time on art or writing or just observing what is around you. You might spend time on meditation, or just being with nature. Perhaps families would have more time to take care of each other and live happily.

However, we live in a culture that wants productivity above almost all else. Productivity is king; being productive provides money to the big people. We tend to like youth and beauty in the USA. When a person is not super young anymore, they become less interesting. The values that are often in older people are similar to wisdom. When a person has reached this age, they tend to learn about the world and start to be able to apply the knowledge they have of the world to their every day and more abstract experience. Youth and beauty are seen as morally good while being a mess or being old are seen as reprehensible.

We have very strict structures around how people would dress in their country. The rules for dressing well haven't changed much in the last hundred years, and when a person is not dressed in the standard of what we perceive to be normal, we find that to be weird and unattractive. Attractive people are actually seen as more intelligent, even though they are not.

Studies have shown that we ascribe traits to certain people who we find attractive. This could be a movie star or someone walking down the street. Either way, we start to view the person as slightly different for being attractive. Part of this is our animal makeup; evolutionarily, men wanted to find women who would be good mates for raising children, and they looked for youth and body type in their search. Women were attracted to mates who could protect them and who had a social status that would enable them to have a good life. This is a structure of evolutionary psychology that still has remnants in our psychology today. It has absences been co-opted by advertising and corporations, and our need to be attractive overtakes us often. When we see an attractive person, we assume that they are more efficient and smarter than someone who may not be as attractive. This is just one example of how we grow up in a certain culture and start to think in the way of the culture.

We have a male-dominated culture, one that celebrates the accomplishment of men and emphasizes male traits. This can affect women and men in several ways. On one hand, women tend not to be traded as fairly in the way that they are afforded opportunities and paid in the workplace. The way that this oppression manifests itself in women is in varying degrees. Sometimes it will include an internalized misogyny and will turn into a stewing heap of resentment. Other women recognize it and work against it. Their struggle to cope with the forces of oppression in their lives will shape the way that there live their lives. Men will also be affected by this society, bemuses men are expected to act a certain way. They are expected to be stoic and tough and never show weakness. To share emotions is to be labeled unmanly. They might find that they need to take special time to learn how to share and express their emotions.

These are all examples of the ways that society faces shape that we are. Peel will have all different types of personalities, no matter their gender or race. But the societal forces that they face will affect the way that their personality is addressed. There are multiple layers that contribute to reading people.

When you are attempting to read people, you should be able to take all of this into account. This means that you should not go from Nebraska and travel to a small island country in the Pacific and expect people to have the same value system as you do. This means recognizing where you came from as a way that you perceive the world and trying to understand that all value systems are objective and that people act how they were taught to act. This might take some time to achieve non-judgmental when you are finding yourself in this problem. Infested of assigning moral good to other groups, try and put yourself in their shoes.

This will require that you use a great deal of empathy, and you will try to learn about a person through the way that they see the world, not the way that you see the world.

There are many different religions, faith systems, attitudes, cultural traditions, and many other differences that distinguish different humans on this planet. However, there are many common connections as well, and there are many ways to understand other people's experiences.

One way to do this is to try food from other cultures. We grow up eating certain kinds of foods, and we usually get used to eating whatever our family ate. This is a great connection woo the world that privies a sense of history and community to the family. This is all great, but it can also be fun to travel somewhere and try to eat the food that they eat on a daily basis. You will start to feel the layout experience the culture a little bit more. There may be restaurants in your town that you never have tired. Try them, and see how it feels to put yourself out of place every once I a while.

Bias is not something that you should beat yourself up over. In fact, it is a way that you can know yourself more deeply and understand how you are interacting with the world. It can be a painful process to come to terms with your own bias, but ultimately, it is something that you will need to face in order to become self-realized. Bias I just a part of the way that we fit into the world.

You also shouldn't convulse your own traditions and values for bias. In our super-woke culture, it is often hip to ignore the old-timey things that our families have done or try to eschew tradition. These people are trying too hard. Traditions are not what hold the bad, regressive views. Traditions need to be upheld; the bad views or olden days can be dropped off without dropping off our culture. Many realize the mistakes of past generations, and they judge them fairly for it. However, we must remember to establish ways that we have cultural continuity and ways that we can come together as a community.

The church used to be a placed of the community the church in the USA and has been declining in membership, in most denominations, for many years. This is because people have more access to information online and they're able to get outside perspectives rather than growing up in a tradition and staying in it lives. Also, people have caught on to the scandals that have been happening in corrupt organizations. The Catholic Church has been mired in scandals of sex abuse for many years. So, people heave goods reasons to leave their churches. What kind of context do we have for the church in 2019? Can it still be relevant?

One thing is for sure, is that the membership of churches is declining and the churches' function as a pace for community gathering has been largely affected. People just don't use the church to go and see their friends and family as much anymore. This could be seen as a good thing, and it could be seen as a bad thing, but either way, it remains true that we haven't yet been able to establish a replacement for this tradition.

This is a big part of modern life for a young person. They are presented with bad options, such as going to a corrupt church or working for a corrupt job, and then they have to take the options because they don't have any other choices. They are forced to do stuff that they don't agree with backs; there are no other options. What really should happen is young people coming to gather to reform the organizations that they have qualms with and preserving the aspects that are good, like the aspects of community gathering and family-like feelings.

Chapter 9: Charisma and Confidence

Many of the positive traits that are known to be part of the Dark Triad personalities have to do with confidence. There are many ways of describing confidence, but it is essentially the courage to be yourself in any situation that might arise. Being yourself might not seem like the classical idea of "confidence," but in fact, it is. Being yourself, whether it is vindictive, happy, or anything else, is what it takes to be confident. Emotions do not weigh down confidence; rather, it uses them for strength. It uses them as coal in the furnace of ambition – fuel for the fire.

A number of things can cause shyness. It could be coming from far back in a person psyche, or it could just be that they are feeling sick today.

Whatever it is, shyness is the state of not wanting to share what is going on with you in the world. It is a state of not sharing with the world, and not knowing how you will be received in the world. This is a state where you are hiding, within your own mind. It is a state of pride and a state or protectiveness.

You must be kind to yourself when you are a shy person. You've got to engage in polite and kind personal self-talk. For example, you can tell yourself, "It's okay. I'm going to be okay. There will be a few awkward moments, and I will make it rough this thing alive." this is the attitude that will help you out. There are thousands, probably millions of shy people in this country. They each have to go figure out their own experiences, but you can know that you are not alone.

One thing to remember with social anxiety is that other people don't really perceive your social system as you think they do. You might be projecting how people see you, and you might think of yourself a person who is awkward. The real fact is that everyone is awkward sometimes.

Social anxiety may make you feel like you don't want to do anything or go anywhere. A big part of learning to deal with this is learning about the anxiety state and learning into modulating your body. The number one way to do this is by breathing. By doing intentional deep breathing, you are able to cause a relaxation response in the body. There are some actions that are intentional, like riding a bike. There are other states that are more automatic, like breathing or blinking your eye. You can, however, decide to do intentional breathing, and you can affect your body's physical reaction by doing this. It is Avery powerful tool for social anxiety. By employing this tool, you can recognize when your body is going to start to go haywire and go; you can do some breathing to calm yourself down.

If there is an event that you are scared to go to, like a party or a show, you can just notice to yourself as you are approaching the event, how you are feeling in your body, and keep checking in every couple of minutes. You will start to notice a tightening, and sometimes it will be in the chest, sometimes in other places of the body. Usually, what is present with social anxiety is a tightening of the chest, a feeling of the heart rate going up, and a feeling of breathing being constricted.

If you are aware enough to notice that you are feeling the symptoms, just know that you can actually change that in that exact moment. You can start to breathe, and you will feel differently. Once you start to take some deep breaths, you should notice that your symptoms decrease.

For some extreme cases, this might not be enough. Some people with s city can be diagnosed with meds that help them to decrease down these symptoms and go to and be healthier in the world. If you have extreme social anxiety, talk to a doctor, and see if there are options for you to take medication.

You don't have to share all of yourself all of the time. In fact, it would be quite strange if you did. You should look to being independent when it feels good to you, and you should know yourself enough to know when you are appropriate in your being shy. This is a natural tendency for many people.

Confidence is the opposite of shyness. Instead of wanting to close everything off and hide everything from the world, it wants to share everything with the world and make yourself known. When a person is confident, they feel that they have nothing to hide. It is a way of being out there in the world, sharing yourself for the benefit of others as well as yourself.

What it really comes down to is being yourself and not being afraid of being yourself. Essentially, we can't change that. We can change behaviors in certain scenarios, and act a certain way around people, and we can make small modifications here and there, but what is truly down there deep within us is whom we are. It is something that is at the core of each person.

So, what is it that keeps us from being ourselves, confidently? It may be that we don't trust ourselves. Some people hold thoughts about themselves that are negative, and they assume that they are not worthy or not as good as others are. It might also be that they hold negative thoughts about the world, and they think that other people and the world are just going to punish them endlessly and that they can never be themselves.

Charisma is when a person is attractive, not just in a physical sense, but in a larger sense. Think about the most charismatic person you know. They are probably able to lead and be a leader. They are probably able to make people feel at home. The thing about charisma is that you are attractive. It means that people want to be around you because they think good things will happen when they are around you. Charisma is deeply tied to confidence because confidence is attractive, but it is something other than confidence. Charisma is a build-up of traits that are adaptive and healthy. People are able to sense a strong and healthy person, and charisma is that collection of attributes.

Chapter 10: Knowing Yourself

The key to being able to avoid manipulation is to know yourself. You will not be able to know yourself unless you experience failure in the world. Most people experience enough failure by the time that they are an adult to really know how they deal with it and learn how to keep on going. If you don't know yourself, you will be used over and over by people who don't care a lick about you. They are just more focused on their own goals. When you know yourself, you are able to know other people better. You will be able to tap into that voice that tells you this is not worth it, that you are being manipulated. If you know yourself, you are less vulnerable to deceit and lies.

This is because people are very self-repressed and they don't learn about themselves. By not learning about yourself, you are opening yourself up to the worst of interactions and relationships. Relationships are shallower when you are like this. They lack depth and concentration. When you know yourself, you are able to analyze what is happening to you and other people. When you know yourself, you are able to protect yourself.

Analyzing people involves keeping knowledge of how we see the world and how we move in the world in order to be able to observe others. This is why knowing yourself is so important. It takes a lot of effort to actually understand how other people see you in the world, and this can cue you into their behavior.

One way to start this is to look at the Enneagram of personality and see what line up mostly with you. This can tell you about the drives that you have in your personality that you might not even realize. When you are trying to find out what type of personality you are, you are engaging in a self-reflexive behavior that will have you to be a better person. If it will help you to know yourself and your intuition will be increased as a part of this.

Another way to know oneself is to participate in the art to watch or listen to the art. A movie can tell us the story of a world. It is a way by which we understand the world. Each time that you talk, you are telling a story, whether it is in words or in the way that you speak the words. This can help to see yourself of the weaknesses and strengths that you have.

When you are reading a great novel, you become immersed in that book, and you get to share a little bit of the writers' world in your imagination. The writer and reader create a continuum, wherein the writer's consciousness is being followed directly by another person. They say that literature is the art that most people can actually escape their world and get into another person's consciousness.

You start to learn the characters, and you start to predict what they are in to do. Characters in the story can be compared to people you know in real life, and the book can give your ideas of own to behavior and change the world in your actions. As you go out through the story, you are experiencing a ride that is the most joyous way of expressing ourselves. This is art.

Art is a mysterious way that we participate in the world. Art has the power to incite wars and peace. It is a way that you can deeply disturb people, and you can keep them happy and calm. Art (we are talking here about the art with a big A, as to mean every category of art, from dance to film to sculpture) is a way that we are in the world that lets us start a feedback loop with the world, and it becomes a source of communication with the world and with others. This is a way that we can find solace and express ourselves to the world.

Art is also a way that we immortalize ourselves. Each human is subject to the lifespan that they are given on this planet, and when you realize when your life is going to end eventually, you start to realize that the world will move on without you. This means that you might be forgotten, at least according to our primal fear. So, we try to do things to counteract this. The most primal and animal way is to have children because then you'll live on in the world through the people who you have created to carry out their own goals and happiness in the world.

Having children is a primal way that people leave a legacy, and it is the ultimate creative act in the world. All other forms of art are underneath this one. That is because art comes from consciousness. That is why humans are not art. We are consciousness, we have the power of gods, and when we create another person, we are using our power as gods. We are also using our power of gods when we create art, but it is to a slightly lesser degree.

Art is a way that you can do an analysis on yourself to deeper levels. Remember the Rorschach test, a way of analyzing people where we look at blobs of ink of paper and say whatever odes to mind first? Well, all art is sort of like that, as a creator and as a viewer. As a creator, when you are creating the art, you are creating the ink blob. Sometimes it is very clear what the artist is talking about. When you look at a Norman Rockwell painting, you understand the scene that he has created because he is putting you right there in a scenario that you can recognize and understand. Other times, the artist is putting you in a place where you can't understand because you aren't meant to. This kind of art can help us to explore what it feels like to other people to experience tarts o fat world. Abstract art is not about telling you things but rather gets you to think.

Many people say that literature is the way that you can most experience another persons' consciousness, out of all of the art forms. Think about the best book you ever read. You were so into it that you couldn't put it down, and when you read it, you were nowhere else except in the world created by the writer. You were a citizen in his world, and there was nothing to do except to be there in the story and experience whatever was going on.

When you do this, you are experiencing a human mode called flow. Flow is when you are just in the moment, when you are only experiencing something that you are doing, like meditating, playing piano, running, driving, or something else. It is a state of focus and a state of creativity.

In order to know yourself, you have to be able to experience the extremes of life. You must have been able to understand the anger and express it. You must know when you feel angry and know what that feels like to you. You must be able to experience joy at the highest level, for this is an extremely human feat. You must be able to take deep pain and failure and also accept the beauty in life. You must be able to immerse yourself in the book and then go pay some bills that you have lying around, which is just menial work that you have to do. There are all sorts of things that you have to deal with that are big and small, and none is less important. It might seem that the small stuff is less important, and in many ways, it is, but the details are something that you can be vigilant with, and they are ways for you to let yourself really experience each part of life.

The number-one way to do this concretely every day and learn about you is journaling. You can journal every day a never write the same thing twice. Journaling doesn't have to be your homework. It can be fun, it can be creative, and it can be a way to release yourself from the shackles of what binds you.

When you write about yourself, you are looking at yourself through the lens of another person, or at least not through your own. By writing about yourself, you are also able to tell your story. Let's talk about both of these aspects of writing.

When you write about yourself, you get to look at yourself through your own eyes, but in a more objective way. Or at least, that's the hope. When you open up the journal and start writing about yourself, and it is all negative stuff, then you should be able to tell yourself that you have a problem there. When you are writing about yourself, try to be as subjective as possible. When you find that you are not able to do this, it might mean that you are too much up in your head.

You see, we start to develop ideas and concepts about ourselves that may or may not be true. Even if they are true, they might not be so good to dwell on. Many people have problems with invasive thoughts or automatic negative thoughts. If you are one of these people, just take your writing and see if you notice these thoughts in writing, and see if you can stop yourself and try to write out thoughts that are kinder and more accurate.

By talking about writing about ourselves in a more objective way, we can get more in touch with ourselves in terms of our real desires, goals, and ways of living. When we are in our heads, we don't get a really good idea of our perceptions vs. the world's perceptions around us. When we are all up in our heads about how we are, the world seems like a movie that we are starring in. When we write about our lives, you are writing a movie. An objective perspective will let you talk about yourself as a friend rather than yourself. You can start to think of this guy or girl as a person who is closer to the world than to your own experience, and when you do that, you reduce the number of feelings and thoughts that might get mixed up with the perspective. When you take out the emotions and thoughts and just go with the facts, you'll find that you can be fairer and more realistic about yourself.

Some people will find that they have self-esteem issues that they need to deal with. Others will be more on the side of narcissism, and they will need to learn about how to reduce their selfishness and start to think more about others.

Telling a story is another big part of writing that is so beneficial to us. Writing a story can really give you some narrative that will let you be expressive and real about your life. Telling the story tells you how you feel about yourself. You can see yourself as a character in a play or movie. What is the character like? Is he or she an antagonist or protagonist? What are the values of the character what are their role in life, and their rod in the story? Once you start thinking of your life in theist way, you can start to be creative about solutions in life, because rather hand thinking about what you would do in the situation, you are actually just thinking about what your character could do, and this opens up many possibilities. Of course, if the character you have assigned yourself is the old, useless man who is not worth anything to anybody, then your story will reflect hat tend your life will reflect that. If you decry yourself as an old but wiry and motivated man, or something more positive, then your story will have all kinds of new possibilities. It is how we view ourselves, that we can see in the story, which helps us to modulate our story, which helps us to modulate our lives.

Of course, knowing yourself and the pursuit of this knowledge must be done with kindness. If you set out to conquer yourself like a distant land for which you have a ruler's disdain, you will find that your campaign incurs more losses than it does gains. You must be engaging in this act in good faith, and you must be ready to be nice to yourself in the process. This is something that can be incredibly difficult for people to understand, and to do it is even more complicated.

There exists a stigma around going to therapy, but this shouldn't stop you if it is something that you feel like you should do. Some people think that therapists are only for crazy and depressed people. That's completely untrue. Therapists work with a proper from varieties of backgrounds, including people from all walks of life.

Therapists can help you determine what they want to work on next in life, and how you should proceed. If you are facing problems, they can help you to develop strategies to learn through the problems and get yourself out of a mess. They can teach you new skills, like breathing or meditation or other coping skills, and sometimes they are just good ear for you to depend on.

One thing that they can certainly do is help you to know yourself better. If you have the means, you might want to see a therapist to accompany your journal, to have someone to process the thoughts with. A good therapist will remain unbiased and supportive with you thought-out the process. There might be people in your life who you know could be supportive to you throughout your day, but a therapist can truly be objective because they're meeting you for the first time when you go in, and they should keep any personal details or feelings themselves out of the process.

One very important part of analyzing people is self-awareness. Before you can go and understand someone else, you must have a deep understanding of yourself in the world. A self-story is a good way to go when you are trying to establish self-awareness. This will involve some introspection. Ask yourself, "Who am I in the world? Where do I come from? What have been my challenges and successes?" When you start to answer this realistically and correctly, you will find level so self-awareness that you did not think you could reach before. If your answer is something like, "well, it did my best in school, and I went to an okay school, and I got a job that is pretty good, and I'm single but pretty happy." This might be a sign that you are not at the level of self-awareness that you want to be at. Try to see if you can get yourself to answer something along the lines of "I am a thirty-year-old man with a good job who has a good time dating, and I love meeting people. I got a good education that west me up for my future. I had an era of difficulty when my dad died, and I try to deal with that every day. But I will get better and better at this." This is an honest answer; this is a person who is very aware of what they are going through and know what to do with themselves. This answer has more confidence and self-awareness. This person feels good about himself or her, and they have built up a sense of resistance to feeling overwhelmed with praise or disgust at him or herself.

Self-awareness can definitely be helped along with exercises. These exercises include reading difficult novels, writing about yourself, journaling, making music or art about oneself, going to therapy, having deep conversations with friends, meeting new people, and many other activates. Some of self-awareness though cannot be found intentionally. This is the area of self-awareness that comes along with wisdom.

See, intelligence is the ability to think and your ability to learn. Information is something that is out there in the world. Data is the raw materials that we observe and see in the world and other people. These factors all come together and when a person is able to use this entire ad actually apply it to their world and know what is going to happen to other people when they do something—that is wisdom.

And wisdom is not something that comes overnight. Wisdom is something that comes with a difficult life and many dark nights of the soul. It is something that has to be earned through tears, sweat, and mistakes. It is something that older people pick up as they go through life because they have seen so much. They have seen so much that they start to be able to understand the world as a big picture rather than trust the small narrow confines of their world.

Sometimes people get into a comfort zone, and they just want to stay in that zone. This can creep up on people, and you have to be intentional about getting out of your comfort zone. This means you cannot keep doing what you are doing. You must do something intentional actually to affect change. There are ways that thou can get out of your comfort zone very easily, in fact.

Another key trait or skill when you are learning to read people is to learn the basic tenets of behaviorism. This means that you understand the conditioned stimuli versus the unconditioned stimuli. Conditioned stimuli, or CS, are when a person or animal is subjected to stimuli that they have learned something from. So, if a dog is presented with a whistle that is associated with getting a punishment, they will know that that means something and this is conditioned stimuli. If a dog is presented with a tasty piece of meat, as it inherently understands it is delicious, they will start to have an unconditioned response, which means they have a physical reaction that has not been taught to them before. The conditioned response is something that an animal is taught to do when presented with a CS. the conditioned response is what the animal is learning, such as the way to navigate a maze to get a piece of cheese.

Reading people takes something in the cognitive sphere, but it also takes seeing able to be self-aware. Being self-aware is being reasonably knowledgeable about yourself and the way you function in the world. It requires knowing yourself, being confident in yourself, and knowing how to question people.

How to talk to people is another basic skill if you want to read people in your verbal communication. If you want to read people, you should ask many questions and be an active listener. Being an active listener means that you are reflecting on what you are hearing, and you are letting the person know that you understand while they are experiencing. It is when you are able to tell yourself what you need to do. When you are an active listener, you are able to hold your attention on a person for extended amounts of time. This is because you are asking questions and trying to read into the person's answers as you are trying to understand them better. This will let you get into their world, and most of the time, a person will let you ask questions because most people like talking about themselves. Most people will do this, but not all will. If you ask them a bunch of questions, some people will ask questions back, or they will be limited in their answers. This can be known as resistance, and when a person is resistant to the conversation, it means that they are not comfortable with talking to you for whatever reason.

Don't assume this reason is you. You might be just getting them at the wrong time of day, or you might have phrased your questing in a way that didn't quite make sense to them. There is a whole host of other possibilities. There might be all kinds of reasons why this person doesn't want to talk right now. Maybe they are just feeling inward, or whatever what you're trying to talk about to them is not something that they want to talk about.
As you engage in more and more of these interactions, you will notice what works and what don't. Test out strategies to see what works most smoothly for you and see if you can find a way to be a good active listener.

When you are a good active listener, you start to become more aware of how your presence affects other's See if you can hold a whole conversation with someone with only asking questions. This will be easier for some to do than others will. When you are just asking questions, you're facilitating another person's thought process, and you are finding information from them as they tell a story.

Each time a person opens their mouth to say something, they are telling a story. It is how we function in the world; it is how we express ourselves, and it is the way that we make peace in the world telling stories lets us know what is like to be human, and hitless us communicative with other humans.

You, then, should go telling your own story. Practice telling yourself the life story in writing. Ask yourself, how did my life start? Where am I right now with my life? When would I expect me to end? What are my major challenges and successes?

Then, you will be able to be a witness to hear other peoples' stories. To be a witness is a privilege. It is something that can help you to become a person who can help others. This is a mode of being that is facilitating another person's telling of their story. Telling stories is therapeutic for the storyteller, or can be, and this is a way that you can help people out.

If you learn to let people tell you their story, then you will be able to read them much better. All you have to do is pay attention to their story and analyze what kind of character they are in their story. They might be the victim, or maybe they are the antagonist. Do they have joy in their story, or is it full of sadness? Do they just talk about their successes, or do they include their challenges as well? These details can tell you lots of information about a person.

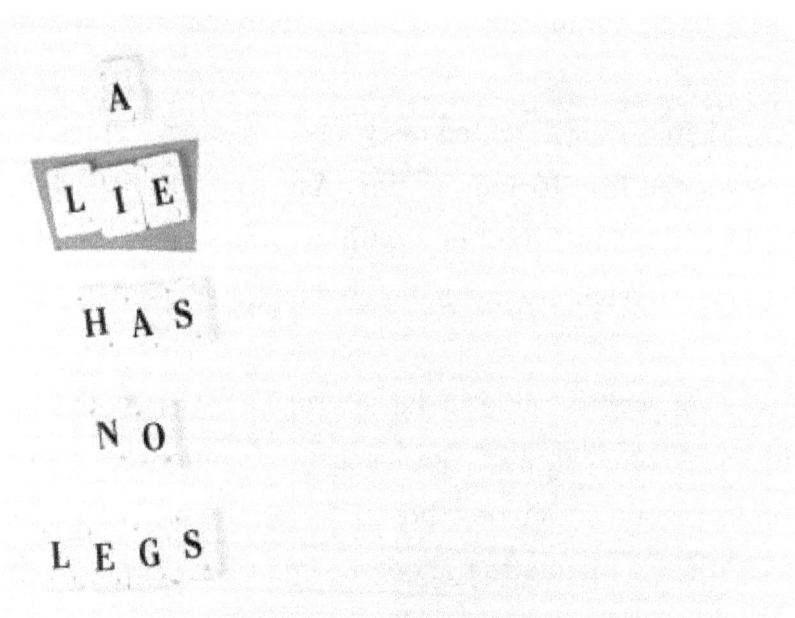

Chapter 11: Spotting a Liar

Lying is a particular human behavior. Lying is not uncommon. Sometimes, it is necessary. There are moral cases to be made for lying in certain situations. People lie for all sorts of different reasons. Sometimes it is to save face, sometimes it is to protect people, and other times, it is to gain something for their own personal good. In any case, being able to spot when someone is lying is a very useful skill. And in order to understand when someone is lying, we must understand human behavior.

In order to delve into how to understand human behavior, we must look to reference the work of B.F. Skinner. Skinner was a hugely important American psychologist who came up with the concept of behaviorism. Behaviorism was his school of psychology, and it has since grown to be one of the most researched and acknowledged schools of psychology. Behaviorism is focused on being able to collect quantifiable data and analyze it in order to learn about the subject. Once data is collected on behavior, then the behavior can be analyzed and changed.

For example, think of a cat that is being trained to ring a bell for a treat. The cat is shown how to physically lift its paw over and over again to hit a button that produces a sound. When the cat is shown how to do this and then given a treat, this is creating approximations of the desired behavior. In this instance, the desired behavior is for the cat to hit the bell and produce a sound. The reared is the treat, which is given when the desired behavior is produced. This creates an atmosphere that supports the behavior with a reward making the cat more likely to begin and continue this behavior on his or her own. There are huge applications to this, in parenting schooling, a nod in the science of behavior in general.

In the above example, the treat acted as a reward for the desired behavior. This can also be known as positive reinforcing, in the context of behaviorism, we don't think about things as positive and negative in a "good and bad" sense, but rather, in an additive or subtracting sense. When you add something to the situation, whether it is a punishment or a reward—that is a positive act. Instead of meaning positive to mean "desired," positive just means that you are adding something instead of taking something away. So, if spankings are administered to make a child know that they aren't allowed to do a behavior, this is actually a positive punishment. This is opposed to a negative punishment, which would be taking something away. A positive reinforce or a positive punishment is when you add something on either end- that is, adding something that is unpleasant or adding something that is pleasurable. Rewards are also known as reinforcing because it reinforces good behavior. A negative reward or negative reinforce would be when you take away something that is difficult or unpleasable when the desired behavior is produced.

Therefore, in the scenario with the cat, you could apply any or all of these strategies. You could apply a positive reinforce, which would be a treat for the cat. You could apply negative reinforcement. This would be something that you have affecting the cat and then when the cat pushes the button (the desired behavior), then you take the bad stimuli away. Maybe this would be something like spraying the cat with a bottle of water until the behavior is produced. This would not work well at all; this is just an example to illustrate the route options of negative, positive, and punishment and reinforce. If you were looking to decrease a certain behavior in the cat, like sitting on the bed, and then you spray the cat with water each time that the cat produces that behavior, you are applying a positive punishment. If you take away the cat's favorite toy when they sit on the bed, you are applying a negative punishment. The most likely option for actually modifying the cat's behavior is positive reinforcement. Positive reinforcement has been studied over and over and has always been shown to be the most successful way of changing behavior. The other methods of applying punishment and reward have repeatedly shown to increase shame and can increase poor self-esteem.

This is all to say that behaviorism is such an important tool in reading people because Skinner has laid out the basic groundwork for a way to understand how behavior works. It is pretty simple in this scheme. A person reenacts behavior that is rewarded. When something is rewarding a certain behavior, people do that behavior again and again. There are also other forces at work, on the punishment side — people, when the punishment for performing certain behaviors, will stop those behaviors, but not always. There are always conflicting forces to be sorted out when applying the principle of behaviorism.

Reading people requires a lot of practice and experience. However, part of harnessing this depends on just being able to tap into the perception and intuition that you already have. One way to effectively tap into your intuition is mindfulness.

You might ask how a higher level of awareness can lead to an increase in your ability to read people. Well, if you think about what it takes to read people, you will find that an awareness of self is important. It lets you know that when you feel angry with a person, you are actually angry and you can have more confidence in yourself that you are expressing the emoting that is actually what you want to express. You can trust your gut more when someone tells you something that might not be true. You can be more in touch with your experience with other people, and they will be able to trust you to be an authentic person. Just by being more authentic, you will be able to read people easier because it is something that draws other people out.

Another part of reading people is making other people feel comfortable enough to share them with you. When a person is anxious or stressed, they do not want to share themselves what others. This becomes a problem when you are trying to read them because you can only read so much into a personal experience without them communicating about it with you. If people are comfortable, they will be more likely to share themselves with you and tell you what's going on with them. This means that you can be non-threatening and supportive and read people much easier as a byproduct.

Behavior is part of the story. It is not the whole story, but it is the most observable thing about a person that we can tell. Some people's behaviors match up with what they feel inside, and others don't. This is a type of congruence that you will need to develop as a person to become self-realized. Some people need to grieve by having a quiet place to share their lives with themselves and only be with their memories than their own body at that moment. Other people have different grieving traditions and needs. Some propel need to celebrate the life of the deceased person, and that is how their grief is expressed: through the celebration of a person's life.

People tend to have different relationships with different emotions. Some people are good at expressing their sadness and aren't good at expressing their anger. Some people are good at expressing their happiness but have difficulty expressing their anxiety. Each person will have to learn which emotions they feel closest to and try to figure out why.

For some people, learning to emote is going to be a big deal. They will have to learn how to express all of the feelings, not just the pleasant ones. They will have to learn how to open themselves up and accept their bodily and cognitive response to an emotion. Other people will have to learn to modulate, control, or decrease their emotions. This is when people have disorders that tend to make them over-reactive to their thinking or acting. They tend to start to be paranoid or start to blame others. This type of thinking is infected by the irrational process of worrying. These include over-catastrophizing, assuming, putting the blame, and looking for an answer that doesn't exist.

What comes out of the relationship that people have with their emotions is a different type of behavior. When people are good at expressing all of their emotions, their behavior will be a certain way. This type of person is fairly spontaneous, expressive, and they might seem a little much to some people. However, these people are learning to let their emotions free in society and letting themselves grow as people. People's behavior will also reflect if they have emotions that they do not express on a regular basis. These will build up and leak out in other ways, rather than being expressed regularly. This is where maladaptive behavior grows. Maladaptive behavior is when a behavior is working toward an end goal, but with the wrong means. What are some examples of maladaptive behavior? Well, all types of maladaptive behaviors can be view as addictions in a way, so lets' start with the maladaptive behavior of an addict.

An addict creates a relationship with a substance because the substance does something for them. It is no secret that a substance, like a drug, will bring people to a differed state of consciousness. Sometimes, it is an upper; sometimes it's a downer. Some people like to use drugs to get them more excited and energized, and others like to take drugs to bring them down. Drugs have very complicated and subjective effects, so this does not mean that there is a binary separation between two types of drugs, but it is an easy way to simplify things.

An addict finds a way to treat a need that they have with a drug. Maybe it's that they feel bored and tired and they want to find something that will let them be excited and energized. Let's say that they start taking Adderall when they are tired. They start doing this when they have a busy workday, and then later, when they have a less busy workday, they are slightly more likely to use the drug. They used it for a need before, why not do it again? It will start to slow down the effects of the drug and the person will start experience things differently. Soon, they feel that they need it. They start to adjust their emotions, behaviors, and thoughts to be centered on whatever can let them get by, and soon, it is not helping them but rather, hurting them.

Let's look at another example of maladaptive behavior. This time, consider a high schooler who is getting in many fights. The child has a need, and that might be to get along with other people and impress peers, or it might be to protect his or herself, or it might be a need to feel strong. Whatever it is, the need is addressed somehow by getting in fights. Maybe it is a badly placed need to interact with others, and the child has not found a way to interact with others in a healthy way. Maybe the kid likes physical activity, but the sports that he has access to are not interesting. There could be all kinds of reason for the acting out. Maybe his family life is very unstable and anxiety-inducing to the kid and so

126

fighting is their way to make sure that they have some control in the world. Whatever the need may be, it is being addressed through fighting; it is just not being addressed in the right way. The kid has learned a maladaptive way to cope.

Let's talk about one more example of pathological or maladaptive behavior. One example of this is when people cheat in relationships. When a person has agreed to be in a relationship where there is intimate exclusivity, and then they go against their word and get involved with another person, they are acting out. There is some sort of need that is not being met in the relationship. Sometimes it is just the sexual need, but this is often not the case. Often with this person, it is a need for attention, for love, or for intimacy that is not being met in the relationship. It could be something as simple as boundaries not being kept that the person has never spoken up to about to their partner. This can create deep problems in the relationships, and even though a person didn't want to, they find themselves violating the boundaries themselves when they are in a situation where it is possible.

All of these scenarios demonstrate how maladaptive behavior can come from the expression of need. It is not what it always appears. This is because of the repression of emotion and thought that we often partake in. When we are not honest with ourselves when we are not fully ourselves, then we start to engage in these behaviors.

Reading people, then, takes this knowledge, and it is able to apply it to everyday life. You can ask yourself about your behaviors and then the behaviors of others: does this behavior take more than it gives? Does the behavior make it worth it to experience the cons of the behavior?" If some behavior is really lacking any real reason to do it, and you're just stuck doing the same old behavior over and over, then that might be a behavior that you should think about trying to modify.

Reading people happens in a split second; it happens when you see a person walking in the door. All you have to do is just trust your gut about the person and then ask questions if you have the chance too. Your ability to read people will be affected by how much you are able to observe from a person. If you see them walking into a room, but they then leave, you will get much less information than if you get to have a whole conversation with them.

When you do get the chance to have a conversation with a person, make sure you are asking questions, and being a good listener. Being a good listener means fully concentrating on what they are saying. You almost have to take it as a gestalt with some people, because you can't hear every single individual word, but you get the overall picture. Sometimes this is necessary. You should look at them in the eye and observe their eye contact. This will tell you about their confidence and directness. You should see how they are standing, how they hold themselves, and how they speak to you. Then, just trust your instincts and keep yourself from getting distracted. Some good tools to use for conversation are reflecting, or saying what the person said back to them, or probing, which is asking about something that they left out. You need to operate on a micro and macro level to read people, and you will need to know the specifics, but also be able to just describe the person in general to the "the vibe." Often a person will have energy; trust your reading of the energy, and know that you are able to go with this gut instinct.

Chapter 12: Detach from Emotions

When tapping into Dark Psychology and its uses, it is important to pay attention to the role that emotion is playing in your decisions. Many of our important decisions will undoubtedly be imbued with emotion. Some of them are relatively easy; others take a great deal of learning and getting through challenges. Often times, we will need to detach from emotions. This chapter is about the situations that drive this need and some strategies to be healthily detached from emotions. Emotions are useful for some things, obviously. They can help you to gain motivation, and feeling joy and pride is one of the rewards for living a good life. Emotions are a necessary and ever-present thing. However, you must learn to separate from these experiences and know that they are not necessarily real. It might be hard to tear yourself away from feeling sad. You might not be able to at all. However, you must learn just to let that experience be. You can't let it take over your entire day. You have to let yourself let go of the "importance" of that emotion.

People who are driven only by emotions are carried away in whatever is happening. They are not able to use the logical side of their brain, rather letting their sadness happiness, joy, or depression take them away somewhere else.

First of all, let's talk about what we're not talking about. When talking about detaching from emotions, we are not talking about becoming cold and disconnected. This can be a source of coping for some people; they become disconnected and "detached" from emotions and use this to be unhealthy and justify it in their minds. This can be described as being aloof. These people are afraid of intimacy and connection. They are afraid of engaging with the world on an emotional level. Of course, we are emotional creatures, and emotions will always be a part of our experience as human beings. We cannot part with this aspect of humanity, thank God. We have to learn to live with our emotions and use them in appropriate ways.

True detachment leads not to disconnection and aloofness, but rather to an ability to be wise. Wisdom is described as the ability to use knowledge. Well, detachment helps along the process of wisdom. We cannot use our knowledge if we rely too much on the emotional information that we are experiencing to make a decision. In order to use the knowledge, we have to make decisions and understand our world, we have to contextualize our emotions. Wisdom comes from this contextualization. True detachment involves acknowledging our emotional states and dealing with them in the most efficient manner. When we are detached from emotion, we are able still to engage in emotion while not letting it take over our decision-making.

We've mostly all heard this one before: "when you assume, you make an Ass out of U and Me." this is an important lesson, and understanding ours and other's biases is a big part of not assuming. As we discussed in the last chapter, understanding biases can help you to realize when you are unfairly assuming something about another person or situation.

The first things to ask yourself when you are thinking about the reason you assume things are this: Are you a psychic? Do you have a crystal ball that tells the past, future, and present truth? I bet not! You may be a psychic with these powers, and if you are, you should disregard this chapter. For the rest of us, it takes to realize that we are not omniscience and that we can't tell what is going on in other people's minds.

We tend to think of more attractive people as more trustworthy. There are scientific studies that show that people tend to have a bias and assume that people who are physically good-looking have good personality traits, more than we would assume for people who are less traditionally good-looking. Why is this? On its face, it seems totally shallow and ridiculous. There is an explanation, however, for this tendency, if we look to evolutionary theory. People used to choose partners based on physical traits that they felt would ensure their survival. So, it follows that men who were the strongest and fastest would find mates and women who were determined the most physically adapted to take care of children and keep the family functional would be chosen. In men, this led to the propagation of certain traits, and a selectiveness for men who are physically tall, powerful, and muscular. For women, this developed into an idealized mate who had a body that appeared fertile and "womanly." However, we are past that now. We no longer need to choose mates that will defend us from the megafauna of the past. We don't need to choose in this way anymore, but we still have vestiges from the past embedded in our psychology. This has resulted in the expectations of gender that we have inculcated in our population.

Another idea to consider is this: you have no idea what another person is going through. Pain and suffering are subjective. Some people hide their pain from the world. They may present as a happy-go-lucky, content person, but really, they have hip arthritis that makes it hard to walk. People may be hiding emotional pain in just the same ways.

We can't assume that we know that people are going through our how they are feeling internally. Sometimes, we will misinterpret a smile or facial expression. If you have some ideas about a person like if they are mad at you, you may see the smallest physical move, as a move of aggression, or you might find that you interpret their speech too hastily for anger.

How do you stop assuming things? You should analyze your thoughts and see when you are assuming and then try to get to the why of assuming. Why are you doing these things? Sometimes, people start the critical thinking process without having all the facets. They may fill in the information into the process that is untrue; to draw conclusions before they can actually be drawn. You can pay attention to how much our mind is doing this; they try to redirect when you are noticing the assumptions. You might find that you have some biases that you had now acknowledged before.

There are three ways of thinking to consider when you are analyzing your thinking. The first is the emotional mind. This mind makes decisions under duress and will be only taking into account the data that is coming from the emotions. The emotional mind will be frenzied, whirling, and unstoppable. It will be passionate and driven by love, art, humor, and romanticism. The next way of thinking is the logical mind. The logical mind is driven to make decisions without any source of emotional data whatsoever. The logical mind can ignore a crying face. It can deny emotion and prove to the world that it has never felt anything, ever. It was a way to self-denial that can be very satisfying for some people. Most people don't make decisions this way, but some do. The logical mind is not good at understanding people in a whole way; it totally relies on scientific observations and quantifiable data. The third, more moderate way of thinking is the wise mind. The wise mind takes into account both the emotional mind and the logical mind when it is making decisions. It addresses the problems of emotionality and the problems of logic. It takes input from both of their perspectives; if the emotional mind is saying something, it listens and responds gently. If the logical mind is making its case, it weighs the importance of logic in that situation. The wise mind is a beautiful synthesis of these two forms of human awareness. IT is called the wise mind because it embodies the wisdom that we see in the most intelligent and efficient people. Often, you will find that older people have more wisdom. This is not true for all older adults, but a lot of them. They have acquired more wisdom simply because they have had more practice in making a decision. Over and over again, they have made decisions. Maybe sometimes they had let the emotional mind take over their decisions, and they saw how that played out. They have also witnessed the ravages of the logical mind, a mind that is disconnected and aloof, and seen the effect that that way of thinking has on their decisions. Often, older wise people are known as "not giving a damn." Simply, put, they don' sweat the small stuff. They have a perspective on life that is influenced by having lived through most of it. They know the importance of emotions, but they also know not to get too wrapped up in it.

Let's face it: it's great to live in emotions. It can be a very indulgent thing. Some people can even enjoy the melancholy sadness that comes with depression .it becomes a certain flavor to your file. There is a certain sweetness to depression, and it can be satisfying, especially for artists and creatives, to live in this sadness and relish it. It feels food for them to be sad. It sounds worrying, but that is the way that we adapt to our lives sometimes. Other people may be more comfortable with the emotion of anger; they will find themselves resorting to angry actions or words to get their point across or get things done. These emotions are states that we hold on to because we feel that they will help us somewhat. Outside of normal emotional functioning, however, there exists the other side to the story the logical mind. The logical mind works with reason and practicality. If you find yourself having trouble detaching from emotion, try embracing the logical mind. The logical mind is what you use when you are scheduling things, doing at problems, or planning a trip by calculating gas mileage. It doesn't need any emotional input to make decisions. However, you must remember that the goal is not to become disconnected and aloof, but rather just detached. Healthy detachment is necessary.

Some people will stand in your way when you try to detach from emotion. Some people want to see you wound up, to see you emotional because they want you to continue the patterns of behavior that you have been engaging with before. Change is hard for people to accept. The people who react negatively to someone being more detached from emotion do react negatively because they are bad people, but because they are people with fears, desires, wants, and needs like the rest of us. This hold not, however, stops you from changing your mindset and behavior in order to more thoroughly detach from emotion.

You see, we each have patterns of thinking, feeling, and behavior. Our patterns get interwoven with the people around us. This can happen in positive and negative ways. For example, there may be someone you often see who you like. They say hi to you, you say hi to them, and you feed off of each other/ energy. This is a great way to have an interpersonal relationship – simple, easy, and low pressure. Another way we get intertwined with people is in our intimate relationships. When we are dating or married to someone, we have a different set of ways that we interact with him or her. For one, you may have a sexual relationship with this person. You may be more honest with this person that you are with other people You might find that yon your relationship with them, you are subject to each other's needs, even physical needs, more often than other people are subjected to them. This is fine and good. Sometimes, however, we get used to accommodating our partner or spouse's need too much, and we take on negative behaviors that accompany or complement others' bad habits. Here's an example: Jane has three sisters. They are loud, boisterous, and fun. She is the youngest. As Jane is halfway through high school, she gets her first boyfriend her sisters all give her lots of teasing about it and makes fun of her from "K-I-S-S-I-N-G" in the tree and all of that. So, this is her first stressor: she feels pressure and anxiety from her sisters, who like to point out a relationship that is new and unknown in her life. Her new boyfriend, Dan, is a sneaky guy. Jane is attracted to Dan's "bad boy" status and often is seen accompanying him on his cigarette breaks outside of school, even though she doesn't smoke. Dan likes that Jane comes with him on his smoke breaks, because he, after all, does feel little unhealthy and ashamed about his habit. So, when Jane starts to be more reluctant about being around Dan when he is smoking, Dan reminds her that "I feel lonely out there, and I don't want to be alone." Jane starts to consistently stay with Dan when he is, and eventually, she picks up the habit for herself. Jane's parents notice her new habit, and they are not happy. They have a long talk with Jane, and they tell her about the risks associated with smoking. They tell her about addiction and about how cigarettes work in the body. Jane understands all this and is convinced that smoking isn't for her. Even though she likes Dan, and wants to be his girlfriend, she doesn't want to smoke. So now Jane has a big problem: first, she has to deal with the teasing of her sisters, but now, she has to deal with the teasing all while starting to modify her behavior. Dan approaches her after lunch on the following Monday and asks her to come outside with him to smoke. Jane decides that she doesn't want to do this anymore, and she tells Dan just that. He starts to go on his diatribe about how lonely and sad it is to be let alone during these times, and Jane starts to feel a little sad for him. She stops, however, and detaches from her emotions. She says to Dan, "I'm sorry that you feel lonely. I have made a personal decision for myself that I don't want to smoke, because of the health risks, and I won't be joining you on smoke breaks anymore. I still like you and want to keep dating." Dan storms off in a huff. However, later, when he thinks it through, he realizes that Jane was honest and mature in her statement. He is able to accept this about Jane and even think about quitting smoking himself.

Conclusion

Thank you for making it through to the end of *Dark Psychology*! Let's hope it was informative and able to provide you with all of the tools you need to achieve your goals whatever they may be.

The next step is to apply these concepts in your daily life and make observations. Just remember, this might be the first step. As you grow more aware of the psychological principles that are happening around you, you will be more powerful in your inner life and also in relationships.

CPSIA information can be obtained
at www.ICGtesting.com
Printed in the USA
BVHW061123140421
604895BV00002B/267